YOU ARE
UNSTOPPABLE
MOVING FROM PAST TO PURPOSE

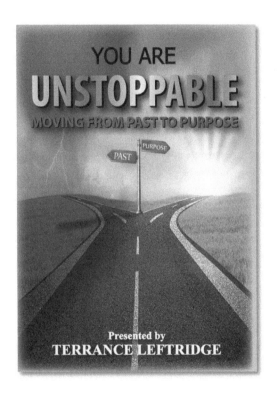

Presented by:

Terrance Leftridge

Copyright Page

Ordering information

Terrance Leftridge

tleftridge@unstoppablecoaching.com

Quantity Sales. Special discounts are available in quantity purchases by corporations, associations, networking groups.

For details contact

Individual Sales- Terrance Leftridge

Includes biographical references and index

Cover creation by Butterfly Grafix

www.butterflygrafix.com

Table of Contents

Introduction

I am THANKFUL for my past and all the trials and tribulations I have endured. I am thankful for losing my first job at Marriot Corporation in the 1990's. I am thankful again for being fired from my "good government job" in 2008. I am thankful for all the failed relationships, all the missed opportunities and all the mistakes I have made along the way.

"Terrance, how is that possible?"

How can you view every firing, failed relationship, missed opportunity and mistake as something to be thankful for? How can you be thankful for the loss of income, the uncertain future, the worry, anxiety, frustration, etc?

Well, I am glad you asked! You see, every event, situation, challenge, circumstance I had to "GO Through" in my PAST (and in your past if you are honest) has provided me with an opportunity to "GROW Through" ...to learn...to become better and to "Move into MY Purpose"! That is why I am collaborating with these UNSTOPPABLE Co-Authors to create this book entitled, "You Are Unstoppable: Moving from Past to Purpose."

Each one of these amazing people is thankful for all the mess they had to go through because it has made them who they are today! In this book, you will read stories of loss and separation. You will read stories of depression and incarceration, both physical and mental. You will read stories of people with overwhelming health challenges. You will read stories of overcoming self-esteem issues and finding Self-Love.

Many of the authors had to "break the cycle" from a belief system that wasn't even theirs! They were raised to think and feel a certain way. This thinking came from parents, relationships formed at a young age or from traditions passed down from generation to generation. These past thoughts stifled them, even paralyzed them from moving into their purpose. But as you take the journey with them in the pages of this book, you will see how finding their "WHY" helped them move past their "Stinking Thinking" into their Purpose.

Each one of these people could have let their PAST take their spirit, their motivation and their desire to live. Being thankful for all the "tests from their past" goes against popular belief and perception. The world teaches us that we should be thankful when things go right, but not when things go wrong. But here is a couple of things I Know:

The Past is a place of REFERENCE, not a place of RESIDENCE.

When you reference your past, 2 things happen. You acknowledge that it IS the past and you either view it as something that continues to haunt you OR as something you have to overcome. When you let it haunt you, then it becomes a residence. This is not a place that any #UNSTOPPABLE person wants to live in. But when you reference the past and see that you made it through, you now can move to another level, the NEXT LEVEL, of your Greatness. You can set up residency wherever you choose knowing that you cannot be limited by the past.

Just because your PAST didn't turn out the way you wanted it to doesn't mean your FUTURE can't be better than you ever imagined.

We all have those "coulda, shoulda, woulda" moments where we wish our past had turned out differently. "I could have studied harder" or "I could have put more into the relationship". You should have asked for that raise or you should have started that business. I am here to let you that your past does not have to dictate your future. It is not too late to have the "the future of your dreams"! It is not too late to find that "dream career" like Marie Cosgrove will share in her story. It is not too late to find "love that extends beyond the walls" like Dan and Tara Gazzuolo found in their story. It is not too late to discover "who you are" and what "you purpose is" like Stephanie Saintyl discovers in her story. As long as you have breath in your body, you have the ability to create the life you want. You could be in store for a future better than you can have ever imagined!!!

A thousand disappointments in the PAST cannot equal the power of one positive action right now. Just Do it.

Authors in this book have had their fair (or unfair) share of disappointments in life and so have I. These disappointments span the length of our existence from childhood up until today. Life isn't fair and that's a fact. As the old folks used to say, "If it hasn't happened to you, just keep on living!" Nevertheless, no disappointment in your past can match the power of one positive action taken today. You are the captain of your ship, the king or queen of your castle! The action you take today can lead you into your "Unstoppable Purpose". As you read the stories in this book, you will see how these authors have done just that. For some of them, it started with one step. For others, it took a series of steps towards "walking in their purpose".

I do not know you or your story, but I do know that it will take the same action from you that they had to take to Move from Past to Purpose. But here's the Good News: If they can do it, you can too! Just Do It!

It is our hope that the stories you are about to read will give you a new perspective on what truly "being thankful for your past" means. We hope you will learn how you can use that as fuel to MOVE you from your PAST into your UNSTOPPABLE purpose!

Terrance "The Unstoppable Coach" Leftridge

Terrance "The Unstoppable Coach" Leftridge has had a desire to help people, empower people and entertain them his whole life. Terrance is at his best in front of an audience. His intent is to always leave people better off than before they met him.

Terrance is a **Certified Life Accountability Coach**. He is the founder of **UNSTOPPABLE Coaching Services Inc.** where the #1 Goal is to help his clients Live Life on the Next Level by partnering with them on their journey to creating, implementing and achieving their visions.

He has worked with men and women who are transitioning from working traditional jobs and helped them start successful careers in entrepreneurship. He teaches them how to be better marketers, better networkers and build stronger relationships that lead to greater exposure and more sales! Throughout his professional career as a coach, Terrance has had a passion for encouraging and motivating people to move to the Next Level of their Greatness.

He has spoken at Live and virtual seminars and training events across the country. He has been the emcee for events featuring **Dr. Ruben West and the Legendary Les Brown**. He utilizes his internet broadcast, **"The Unstoppable Stories Show with Terrance Leftridge"** as a platform to expose his guests to a larger audience and as a result increase their circle of influence and generate leads.

For more information on booking Terrance for your next event or speaking engagement, contact him at **Terrance@unstoppablecoaching.com**.

<u>Introducing Marie Cosgrove</u>

People in your past may have made you feel unworthy of success because of your circumstances. People in your past may have teased or talked about you because of a disability you had. People in your past may look down on you because of situations beyond your control. It probably has affected your self-esteem and your confidence. Nevertheless, if you have the FAITH and BELIEF to rise above that negativity, Unstoppable Success is especially sweet!

Author Marie Cosgrove knows what it feels like to be called unworthy. By all accounts, she wasn't even supposed to be here! She was not supposed to be born because doctors felt her mother would not be able to take care of her. She was not supposed to be able to learn because she was the child of a brain-damaged mother. She was not supposed to find love because for most of her life all she knew was abuse. She was not supposed to be able to have a career because she did not have a college degree.

However, what Marie did have was a *Wellspring of Life* that allowed her to pour Belief and Faith into a heart that once only knew death and depression. When you read her #UnstoppableStory over the next few pages, you will discover how she used her WHY to fuel her fire to succeed. She did not allow negativity from people, places or things to deter her. She has gone on to achieve Greatness against all odds and wants to share with you how she went from Homelessness to CEO to Living the Unstoppable Life.

As you read her #UnstoppableStory, look at your own story and see if you can recognize how Belief and Faith have allowed you to get to where you are today.

~ Terrance Leftridge

CHAPTER 1

The Wellspring of Life

Imagine if you only had economic prosperity. If you only had good looks. If you only had an education, or the intelligence to obtain a higher level of education. If you only had a perfect family. If you only had perfect health. If you only had_____ (fill in the blank).

Consider you were born with all the advantages, such as intelligence beyond your years, economic prosperity, perfect health, perfect looks, yet you still suffered from spiritual deficiencies, depression, a feeling of pitifulness, self-destructing thoughts, and felt mentally starved.

Unfortunately, many who have found success, prosperity and fame have also struggled with a lack of self-worth and self-destructive behavior. All one has to do is look at some of Hollywood's most envied stars. Hollywood stars are coveted for their looks, economic status, and fame. For example, Halle Berry once stated, "I was sitting in my car, and I knew the gas was coming when I had an image of my mother finding me."[1] She attempted to end her life, even though she was already one of the most successful actresses in Hollywood.

Now, suppose you were not born into wealth or a perfect family. Are you destined to failure? A miserable life? A life without an Unstoppable Purpose? Absolutely not! Can you have an Unstoppable YOU? Absolutely!

Unfortunately, at one time, I thought failure was my only option. I will share with you how I overcame my self-destructive thoughts and how you too can overcome and unleash the Unstoppable You that you are.

First, I will share with you what was holding me back. One of my most significant setbacks was labeling myself a victim (I call this a bad case of victimitis). The victimitis disease struck me with a vengeance. I was born into poverty with no father and a mom who suffered permanent brain damage, whom many called "crazy."

My mother, Mary, was in a severe car accident while traveling to Durango, Mexico from the United States for a wedding. She was only 22 years old. My grandfather was driving on a straight and narrow road for many hours. Suddenly, there was a sharp curve, known as "La Esquina Del Diablo" (The Devil's Corner). There was no sign indicating the sharp curve was approaching. My grandfather drove off the road over the curve, hitting a tree. My grandmother broke both of her legs. My uncle, who was two at the time, flew from the back seat of the car through the windshield and landed on the hood of the car. You could not see his face because it was full of blood. All you could see was the whites of his eyes. He also broke both of his legs.

Fortunately, my aunt, who was also traveling with them, had no injuries. But my mom's head was crushed. The only people who stopped were looters who took all the family's belongings. It would be 24 hours before the family was finally rescued. A pickup truck stopped, and the driver agreed to take them to the closest hospital.

My grandfather, grandmother, and uncle rode in the bed of the truck, while my aunt and my mom rode in the front with the driver. By this point, my mom was unconscious with blood spewing out of her mouth and head. My aunt was trying in vain to stop the bleeding with her hands.

At the hospital, the doctors said, "Mary is lucky she is still alive, but she has severe bleeding in her brain. She won't live much longer."

My grandmother, however, did not believe in luck, she believed in something much greater.

She told the doctors, "You must perform surgery to stop the bleeding!"

The doctors replied, "Surgery is way too risky, and could result in immediate death or a permanent vegetative state. Besides, there is no doctor on staff skilled enough to perform the surgery. We will have to call in a surgeon from another city. By the time he arrives Mary will be dead." My grandmother insisted on the surgery, regardless.

Two months after the surgery, my mother remained in a coma on life support, with a breathing tube in her throat.

The doctors said, "It's time to pull Mary off life support. There is no chance of recovery."

My grandmother refused to accept the prognosis and demanded they send my mom back to the States. In the United States, the doctors gave Mary the same diagnosis and stated that they would have to take her off life support. My grandmother put her faith to the test and insisted on one more day. On that one extra day my grandmother fought so hard for, my mom miraculously opened her eyes. She had to learn how to walk, talk, and do everything all over again. She did have brain damage, but she was going home.

My grandmother's faith was soon put to the test yet again. One night, while my mom was out with friends, she was raped, and it resulted in pregnancy.

The doctor told my grandmother, "This baby must be aborted. There is no way the baby will be born 'normal' with all the medication Mary is on. Plus, think of the shame that will come upon the family having a child out of wedlock."

During that era, it was considered shameful to have a child out of wedlock—especially a child conceived via rape.

My mom told my grandmother, "God saved my life, and I'm not going to take it away from my baby!"

"I will help you raise your child," my grandmother told her.

Photo of my mom, Mary, before the accident.

Today, I can see the blessing in the fact that my grandmother and my mother decided to give me a chance at life, but I didn't always.

Today, I know that life doesn't have to be perfect to be fulfilling.

With the miracles that took place, you would think that I would have appreciated life and that it would be a smooth ride after what my family experienced, but it wasn't.

I was bullied by certain family members who would say, "You are not part of the family. You do not have a father; you are a bastard child. You are cursed."

Children would not play with me; they would say, "My mom told me not to play with you because your mom is 'crazy,'" not realizing my mom had brain damage.

I was the one kid who was never invited to birthday parties or friends' houses, nor did they want to come to my house and play. I hated recess because I would sit all alone, watching the other kids play.

The first five years of my life, I lived with my mom, after that I went to go live with my grandma, and would stay with my mom on weekends, school vacation days and summers.

Because she had brain damage, she lacked a moral compass. She would often bring strangers into her home who would abuse me in unimaginable ways, too grotesque for me to even discuss here. I still remember the day I moved from my mom's house to my grandmother's house. I was only five years old when I was picked up by the policemen and driven to my grandmother's house. My mother had left me alone that night, and I was scared, so I dialed '0', which in those days connected you to the operator, who sent the police over to pick me up.

Growing up without a father, with a mother who had brain damage, and with a childhood filled with violence and abuse led me to believe that there was no greater purpose for my life. I was destined for failure. After all, I was told I was too dumb because I did not fully develop in my mother's womb. In school, I was taken out of class in the mornings to the portable buildings. The portable buildings were where the mentally challenged students were taken after roll call.

When my name was called to leave the main classroom, the kids would laugh and jeer, "She is crazy just like her mom; she has to go with the dummies!"

I recall feeling worthless because I believed I was too dumb to learn. I was a bastard child and I had been violated and abused, which left me feeling dirty and worthless. The decline in my mental attitude followed me through adulthood. I married young, at the age of 18, and had three beautiful children. At the age of 21, I had a son. At the age of 22, my only daughter was born, and by the time I was 24, I was pregnant yet again. My ex-husband had a violent temper, and our marriage ended in divorce, which was finalized the week my third son was born.

The court ordered that my ex-husband could see the children under supervised visitation four hours every other weekend. However, I was awarded a permanent protective order, and he chose not to see the children during the four hours he was allotted. I was left to raise my children alone as a single mom.

At work, though, I was successful. I was successfully running the marketing department of a financial institution and greatly contributed to the growth of the bank from two locations to seven within a short period of only two years.

I married again within two years of my divorce to a successful businessman, who became involved in the church and seemed like a great person. I truly was not ready for the relationship, but I did not have the self-confidence to say no to marriage. I was told by family members and friends who encouraged me that it was the right thing to do.

They said, "You can't raise those children alone. They need a dad. Here is God bringing someone into your life who can help you, and you would be very selfish if you declined to marry him."

Sadly, the second marriage was worse than the first. I had one child with my second husband, and it quickly ended because he abused my kids in much the same way I had been abused, but worse. He lost all parental rights to the one son we had together. It took many years to overcome my sense of guilt and depression over the choice I had made to marry a man who abused my children.

I continued to thrive in business, though. By this time I was managing a $400 million marketing budget for a Fortune 150 company—and without a college degree.

Unfortunately, because of the serious abuse my daughter experienced and witnessed, she was suffering from post-traumatic stress disorder (PTSD) at the young age of five. My oldest son, who was seven at the time, was suffering from

JDMS (juvenile dermatomyositis), a rare autoimmune disease, in addition to rheumatoid arthritis and other serious medical issues. The doctors didn't expect him to survive past his 18th birthday.

Today he is approaching his 26th birthday and is successful and healthy. At the time, however, I had to give him weekly shots, take him to daily physical therapy sessions, and take my daughter to weekly counseling for her PTSD. With all the doctors' appointments, I was unable to keep my job and was forced to resign so that I could focus on my children.

One of my sons and me on the living room floor where we would sleep along with my other children.

The medical expenses were very high, which made it difficult to support my four little ones. I simply could no longer afford my home and car. I ended up losing everything and becoming homeless.

My aunt and uncle agreed to let me stay in their humble home. Unfortunately, the only space available for my children and me was the living room floor. We slept on and played on that floor and called it home until I could find a job that would allow me to raise myself up off the floor and into a place of our own.

I came across an ancient text that had a profound effect on me, it was written by a wise king named Solomon.

"Above all else, guard your heart, for it is the wellspring of life."[1] Proverbs 4:23 NIV

In my heart, I was worthy of beatings because I was a bastard child. I felt dirty, shameful and ugly on the inside. How could I ever be clean again after all the abuse I experienced throughout my childhood and my marriages? Besides, I had no father; my life was the result of a very violent and serious crime. I was a mistake. Why should my heart be worthy of guarding?

But, Scripture says that the heart is the WELLSPRING of life.

Was I spewing out "death" instead of life? Had my heart become so darkened that I was refusing to allow "the wellspring of life" to flow in and through me?

I wanted this "wellspring of life" to flow through me so badly. What if I changed what was in my heart? Could it be possible that if I simply made this one small change I could be much, much more, a different person even? A new person. A person of value. A person of character. An Unstoppable Me. A wellspring of life. Wow. I wanted this wellspring to spring forth in me a new heart.

Below are some exercises I did that perhaps will help you identify some of your key strengths that will help you bring forth the fruit from your very own wellspring of life.

First, I took the time to list the things I did well, areas of life I was good at. All of us have something to contribute, something of value and something we are good at.

1) What do you do very well? List three or more things you do very well.

1 _____

2 _____

3 _____

Note: Everyone faces criticism from others, sometimes daily. Sometimes, criticism comes from those you love most. Other times, you hold on to past criticisms and carry them around like a souvenir.

Challenge: When you remember an old criticism, throw out that thought and replace it with a new thought. Remember those things you do very well. When you receive destructive criticism, let it go "in one ear and out the other." In other words, don't dwell on that criticism. Focus on what you do well.

2) How often do you think of your past experiences?

a. As soon as you become aware that you are thinking of a past painful or hurtful memory, think of where you are right now.

i. Are you safe? (If the answer is no, get to safety immediately by calling 911 or your local shelter).

ii. Are you healthy?

iii. Are you OK, right now?

Think on this:

"Whatever is true, whatever is noble, whatever is right, whatever is pure, whatever is lovely, whatever is admirable—if anything is excellent or praiseworthy—think about such things"[2] Philipians 4:8 NIV (it is a text from one of my favorite books written by Paul, the apostle).

Example: Every morning, I was filled with grief about the abuse my children experienced. I did not want them to see me depressed. So, I would go to the restroom, lock the door, and turn on the shower so they could not hear my tears and my painful cries. My heart was so very hurt, and the pain I experienced was beyond anything I could accurately describe. I was dwelling on the past, dwelling on their pain, and asking God, "Why? Why did you allow this horrible, horrible thing to happen to my innocent children? Why God? Why?"

I realize that we live in a world where we all have free will. What this means is that whatever action you take will have a consequence on another person, whether negative or positive. For instance, if you are at a restaurant and an evil person comes in with a gun and begins shooting, the good people in that restaurant will be impacted by the evil person's actions. If we did not have free will, we would all be robots and would not have the freedom to choose between good and evil. Sadly, when people choose evil, it often impacts those who choose good.

I began to thank God for bringing us to safety. I was thankful that the abuse was now over. The children WERE safe now. We had a roof over our heads—even though we were sleeping on the living room floor, we were not out in the cold under a bridge. I gave thanks for the little things we did have. We had each other. The children were both a gift and a blessing. I looked at what I did receive from the "hell" we all lived through and that "hell" produced four beautiful lives.

3) What are ten things you are grateful for today?

Challenge: Every day, write down ten different things you are thankful for.

I make a list every day to this day. It seems so simple, but it is powerful. Within 30 days, if you follow this simple plan, you will experience a transformational positive mental attitude, despite your adversities.

Sometimes the most beautiful experiences in life come out of adversity. You may not fully understand the adversity you are facing, but you can trust and have faith that you will see the beauty in the end. Look at your adversity as going through a "learning vortex"—when you get out, you will be astoundingly stronger. If you have survived a storm, tornado, or hurricane you are bound to come out stronger on the other end. Adversity has a way of making us stronger and more powerful—unleashing the Unstoppable You and the wellspring of life that is within you.

CHAPTER 2

From Homeless to CEO

Many people ask how I became CEO of a medical diagnostic device manufacturing company.

First, I will share with you the journey I took to get there. Not having a home or a car and caring for four little ones while we all slept on the living room floor was not easy. Additionally, my aunt and uncle were growing tired of my daughter's non-stop crying in the middle of the night. Beginning around midnight, she would wake up screaming and crying so loud, it caused everyone in the home to wake up. She would toss and thrash, throwing and kicking her legs around so hard that it was impossible for anyone to hold her. This would continue until 3:30 or 4:00 am every single day. The counselors said it was a result of the abuse she had experienced.

My aunt and uncle were having difficulty getting enough rest in the evenings. It was taking a toll on the entire family, as no one was getting rest. When my daughter would cry, my baby would wake up crying too. Then I had two children crying at the same time.

I needed a solution, and I needed one fast.

Mark, an apostle in one of my favorite books, wrote, "Therefore I tell you, whatever you ask for in prayer, believe that you have received it, and it will be yours."[1] Mark 11:24-25 NASB Belief is different from wishing. You can't wish yourself into a CEO position. You can't wish yourself a millionaire. But, you can believe and have faith that you can become a CEO. You can have faith that you will become a success.

A friend of mine who was kidnapped as a teenager and force into the sex slave industry escaped five years later. She had a strong desire to create plays as an outreach program for at-risk youth. With unwavering faith, she went to the Victoria Theatre in Dayton, Ohio and asked to schedule her play.

The person who ran the theater told her, "This is the Victoria Theatre. We only allow top plays to perform, such as *Wicked*, *The Lion King*, and *The Phantom of the Opera*. Who are you? Are you a producer? Have you ever put together a play? Are you an author? You are nobody. You can't have a play here in this theatre."

Her faith was too strong to let anyone tell her no. She insisted. They told her she needed a minimum of $5k to put down to secure a date for her play. They laughed thinking she would not come up with the money. Within two weeks she was able to raise the money. Today, her plays sell out at every show.

I too put belief into owning my own home, car and getting a job to get my children off that floor we were living on!

I began to look for part-time jobs within the marketing field since that was where I had plenty of experience. Unfortunately, only full-time jobs were available, and with all the weekly medical appointments, I knew I would not be able to maintain a 40-hour-a-week work schedule.

Then I had an idea. With a sales job, I could negotiate a commission structure and work my own hours, if I met the respective company's required quota. At first, I faced many rejections because I did not have a college degree or experience in selling. Finally, I was offered a job at a radio station, but they insisted on a salary plus commission compensation package. I pleaded with them to allow me to work straight commission and prove to them that I could exceed their quotas if they gave me an opportunity. The salary would tie me down to putting in 40 hours a week; time I did not have.

They said they had never heard such a request. Their company had a policy, and they could not deviate from that policy or the terms of the offer. Therefore, I had to decline the job because I needed to be available for my children's doctors' appointments.

Surprisingly, I received a call from a friend of mine, Dr. Rammamurthy, who said, "Marie, a guy stopped by my office asking if I knew of a marketing person. He said he drives four hours every week to this territory, and he is tired of the long drives; I told him you were the best marketer in town."

I called the guy right away. We met at a restaurant, and I took along my portfolio of the marketing work I had done for financial institutions; insurance companies, including USAA; and other companies, such as The American Heart Association, FedEx, Sprint, etc.

He started laughing. "Little girl, this is not marketing. This job is sales. You don't have what it takes to sell thirty to eighty thousand dollars worth of equipment. What do you know about sales? Have you ever done sales?"

My reply was, "Yes, I have plenty of experience in sales. I had to sell the board directors on how to spend a four hundred-million-dollar budget. Thirty to eighty thousand is a drop in the bucket compared to four hundred million."

He said, "OK, I will agree to let you speak with my boss. But the example you gave me is NOT really sales."

The next day, the VP of sales called me and asked, "What experience do you have?"

I shared with him my experience and the value I could bring to the company. He said he could not take the risk with someone who had no actual experience selling. I told him there was no risk to him if I paid for my own training.

To get money for training, I approached various doctor's offices I had connections with through the financial institution I had worked for and the freelance marketing I had done and picked up a few projects. This allowed me to earn enough income to pay for a babysitter and my training. I had the faith to believe that I would receive a home and car and be able to fulfill all of my children's needs. I did not have a choice. I was never, ever going to rely on anyone to help me raise my children. I would never put them in a dangerous situation again. I was going to take control and claim authority over plenty. I have a strong belief in a God who states that, "He has plans to prosper you and not to harm you, plans to give you hope and a future." Jeremiah 29:11NASB I was not letting go of the hope and future that was mine. Hope and future belong to you too. YOU are Unstoppable!

At training, I did well. I listened and learned about how the devices the company manufactured helped millions of patients suffering from debilitating diseases, and that they could find relief and healing. I was excited to be a part of the process of helping patients. I passed all of the tests given to me after each lecture.

Despite my success, the president walked over to me at the end of training, in front of 40 executives, among whom I was the only female and minority, pointed his finger at me and said, "Listen, little girl, you are never going to make it in this industry. Face it, with your little girl voice you couldn't make it in this male-dominated industry. The most you will ever sell is candy. Go home."

"Oh, yeah? Watch me! Give me thirty days, straight commission. You have nothing to lose," I replied. I went home with a thirty-day contract, and I was excited to prove him wrong.

When I got home, I found that my grandfather who helped raise me had been diagnosed with leukemia. I had 30 days, but I had no idea how much time my grandfather had left.

I stayed by his bedside every day at the hospital. Three weeks later, my grandfather passed away. I received a call from the president the week my grandpa passed away. He said, "Little girl, we are canceling your contract! Your time is up, and you have not made a single sale."

My reply was, "My time is not up, I have one week left." I called on many doctor's offices that week. The door slammed shut on me every day.

On Thursday of that week, I received a call from one of the doctors I had called on earlier in the week.

He said, "Meet with me tomorrow at noon at my office regarding your products."

I met with him at one of his six locations—the newest one. The furniture had not yet arrived. I sat on his stool, which he had warned me about.

"Be careful and don't slip. It is a bit slippery."

Well, after my presentation, I slipped off the stool, and the stool shot back. I fell flat on my back with my two feet sticking straight up.

He came over and asked me if I was okay. He either felt sorry for me or I did a great job in my presentation. I walked away with enough to cover my quota for the next *three* months. Of course, I called the president right away to let him know about the sale.

His reply was, "Let's see if the check clears."

To the president's surprise, I became the #1 national sales representative in the nation. Unfortunately, after successfully working for them for a year, I received a notice from the manufacturer of the equipment I was selling stating that the distribution company I was working for was no longer authorized to distribute the products. I was offered a hefty increase in commission if I would become a distributor.

The distributor threatened me, along with every other representative, with a lawsuit if I sold directly from the manufacturer and violated the contract we had signed. Some salespeople took the risk and went to court. I could not afford a lawsuit at that time, so I walked away and stopped selling the product.

I began selling a completely different product in another field of medicine for another manufacturer. I quickly became the #1 salesperson in the nation. I did exceptionally well and was able to get out of debt.

Unfortunately, I received a devastating call. "You are making too much in commission. You are not a doctor. You are not an engineer. You have no qualifications to allow you to earn the amount of money you are earning. We are going to put you on a salary."

The salary was much less than what I could earn on commission, making it impossible to support my family as a single parent, and I had no financial support to turn to. I declined the offer and was subsequently fired.

Again, I was left without a job. I could have resorted to a victimhood attitude or victimitis. After all, here I was, a single mom of four without a job. But I'm UNSTOPPABLE—just like you.

In the previous chapter, I talked about how it is essential to think about the things you are good at and your past successes. I began to look at life from the perspective of what I already had. I had already been the #1 national sales representative in the nation for more than one company. I wrote a long list of accomplishments, which is what you will need to do for yourself as well when you are at rock bottom.

With my built-up self-confidence, I started my own company and built it into a very lucrative and successful world-wide company. Two years later, I purchased the company I that had fired me for refusing their lesser salary. I turned it into an employee-owned international company.

However, success in business was not my passion. I wanted to reach out to others who had faced the same challenges of overcoming abuse, violence, and despair—some of the same difficulties I previously faced. Youth who had been written off. Youth whom people said there is no hope for. I could relate because I, too, was once one of those youth others said there was no hope for.

I recall one particular young man. I was told he was both physically and emotionally abusive to his mother and would beat her. This young man attended my six-week mastermind, based on the book *Sometimes You Win, Sometimes You Learn, for Teens* by John C. Maxwell, along with a group of other teens in the juvenile system.

He attended every session, completing all six weeks of the mastermind. Later, I was surprised when I got a letter from him stating that, as a result of the mastermind, he not only no longer raised his hand to hit his mother, but he also no longer raised his voice towards her and he now respected her.

All kids are reachable, teachable, and redeemable. Young people are 27% of our population, but 100% of our future. I am blessed to have been mentored personally by many of the greats—Brian Tracy, John Maxwell, Les Brown, Bob Proctor and Paul Martinelli—who continue to commit to training me and others so that we can be instruments of change and equip others to be Unstoppable.

My passion is working with inner-city youth. What is your passion? Whatever your passion may be, know that you have it within you to be a catalyst for change and be Unstoppable. As Zig Ziglar said, "See you at the top!"

Notes

The Wellspring of Life

1.   Berry Talks About Suicide Attempt. Accessed December 4, 2017. http://articles.chicagotribune.com/2007-03-30/news/0703290817_1_gabriel-aubry-eric-benet-halle-berry

2.   Phillippians 4:8 NIV – Finally, brothers and sisters. Accessed December 4, 2017. https://www.biblegateway.com/passage/?search=Philippians+4%3A8&version=NIV

From Homeless to CEO

1.   Mark 11:24-25New American Standard Bible (NASB). Accessed, December 4, 2017. https://www.biblegateway.com/passage/?search=Mark%2011:24-25

2. Jeremiah 29:11New American Standard Bible (NASB). Accessed, December 4, 2017. https://www.biblegateway.com/passage/?search=Jeremiah%2029:11

<u>Meet Marie Cosgrove</u>

 Marie Cosgrove is a successful entrepreneur with a proven track record of turning failing companies into Million dollar profit centers.

However, prior to her entrepreneurial success, Marie became homeless after having to quit her job to care for her four small children, two of which had serious medical conditions, causing her to lose her home and car.

She eventually lifted herself from homelessness to #National Sales Rep.

Unfortunately, she was fired, but two years later, she purchased the same company she was fired from and became CEO.

Marie serves as President Advisory Council on the John Maxwell Team and is mentored by the Number One Motivational Speaker in the World, Les Brown. She is a Certified Facilitator Instructor in the Round Table Method, Certified Human and Behavioral Coach. Marie also serves as President of the Board of Directors for Imagine Public Charter Schools in Dayton, OH.

<u>Introducing Lady Reshell Dotson Matheny</u>

Imagine with me if you will being alone in a quiet room and all you can hear is *Drip, Drip, Drip.* It is a sound we take for granted when we are involved in the hustle and bustle of life. While life is good, carefree, and filled with a thousand other distractions, you may never notice the drip at all. When you finally notice it, you wonder is it coming from the kitchen sink or may be the bathroom. You hope it is not coming from a leaking or broken pipe because you know that could be a BIG problem! You jump up from whatever life has you doing at the moment with the sole intention of making the *Drip* stop!

Lady Reshell Matheny had many days like this when she wished the *Drip* could stop or even would stop. However, the drip she heard was not coming from the kitchen or the bathroom. It was not coming from a leaking pipe, but she was dealing with a BIG problem! As you read #HerStory, hopefully you will see what it means to be POSITIONED FOR PURPOSE even when everything around you seems to be DYING INSIDE.

Your relationship may be dying. Your career choices may be dying. Your dreams for the future may seem like they are dying and inside of you your spirit may be dying as a result. However, just realize that a greater work may be at hand. You see the one thing I know is that just when I think nothing is happening, GOD is up to something. He knows that sometimes you have to let a few things DIE so that you can live.

Lady Reshell has a #UnstoppableStory of personal reflection, mindset correction and #Warrior transformation. She will show you what can happen when you find you find WHY and the "source" of your WHY! If you let it, I am sure this story help you move from your past into your purpose.

~ Terrance Leftridge

Chapter 3

POSITIONED FOR PURPOSE

Keymo Dayzze
(Chemotherapy Days)

Aching bones, loose teeth, chocolate skin,
what the hell is happening?
Black fingernails, smelling of crusty sores
wondering how much more.

Toxins dripping into my veins, hour after hour,
waiting to kill cells is enough
to drive anyone insane.

The pain of sores in my mouth has caused me
to lose weight and look paper thin.
No appetite, no relief in sight.
I can't fathom why this journey began.
Trying to hold on when I have every reason
to let go.

Seeing those little eyes looking up at me
brings me to my knees, praying and
asking my heavenly Father to preserve me.

Growing old, wanting to see my seeds in bloom.
Popping pills, hoping to eliminate the residue.

Finding strength, I never knew I had.
Life goes on until the good Lord sees fit.
Celebrating life day by day as my beauty
fades away.

Hair shedding like rain falling immensely from the
sky,
the rain hides my tears as they disappear into thin
air.
Paralyzed by the collateral damage,
searching for a better tomorrow.

Blood running thin, so the doctor
had to pump some more in me.
Life has a way of humbling you to bring
you to praise.
Praise for the things past, present and future.
Knowing what's to come is better than
what's been.

Keeping hope on these sleepless nights.
Waiting on an encounter with God to bring
relief in sight.
Mind racing, physically dying inside

while the storm
attempts to drown out my faith.

I hold on with all my might.
Praying to my heavenly father
to erase the stain of these
keymo dayzze.

DYING INSIDE

"Drip, drip, drip" was the sound bouncing off of the bag filled with toxins seeping into her tiny veins. In and out of consciousness, her eyes were swollen shut, her breathing shallow, all the while gasping for air. Chest rising with every breath taken that seemed to leave her exhausted. Tubes with fluids attempting to wipe out the bad cells were attached from every direction. You see, this was her first day of chemotherapy after finding a lump in her right breast on top of everything else wrong with her health. As she fearfully fought to survive, the cells continued to divide, eventually contributing to her demise. She was my mom's firstborn and first buried into eternity, to rise again to be with our heavenly Father. *R.I.P., Nancy R. Marshall, 12/9/10.*

Nancy was the first *BIG* loss for our close-knit immediate family and it really took a toll on us. We knew she was sick and had many close calls but, somehow, she'd always pull through because that's what fighters do. The family didn't address her illness other than to meet with the doctors to inform us of her grim prognosis. Where did it come from? Diabetes and high blood pressure were prevalent in our family. The "BIG C" had never been spoken of before because there was no need to. There were only two family members with breast cancer before my sister was diagnosed. One of my mom's second cousins who died in her 90s, and an aunt on my father's side who is alive and in her 60s today. No one talked about our risk. It was like we deemed their diagnosis as some isolated incident and it wouldn't happen to the rest of us. After all, it didn't run in our family.

It never entered my mind that God was positioning me and giving me a glimpse into my painful future. Now, three years later after my sister's death, I was the one leaving the doctor's office with the dreaded diagnosis, and the elevator ride seemed like an eternity.

My mom on one side of me said, "Can you hear the chains falling in the spirit?"

I said "No," while in total disbelief.

The three dreadful words that played over and over in my head were all I could hear loud and clear. *YOU HAVE CANCER!* And my next thought was, *YOU ARE GOING TO DIE.*

All I could feel at that very moment was anger. Who was I angry at? I couldn't decide if I was angry at myself or at God. The dreadful question came to mind, *Why ME?* I don't drink or smoke, and I'm not overweight. I'm a very active person who was conscious about what I ate and exercise, so what in the HELL went wrong and why? Was God trying to get my attention?

I had to somehow pull it together because I didn't want everyone to know. A feeling of shame came over me as if I did something to deserve this diagnosis. Many will question, "What did you do to deserve or cause this?" until it happens to them or someone they love. I've found that no matter how much you think you know about cancer, having it and dealing with the many gifts it brings is a whole new world that many of us would rather not enter into. A world filled with uncertainty, changes, and hope. Hoping that this is all a bad dream, and when I wake up, I will be whole again.

As my doctors worked on putting a plan together on how I was going to fight this, I couldn't help but think, *I am going to die.* Death was unavoidable. I was witnessing so many people losing their battle and family members left with unanswered questions. The fear in me became so overwhelming. I began questioning God.

Where is God?

What kind of God allows this horrible disease to consume so many?

Why hasn't God allowed a cure?

Does God take pleasure in seeing us suffer?

Am I really healed by His stripes?

Do I allow the doctors to poison me in order to get rid of the devil that was attacking (me) physically, mentally and spiritually as well as raping me financially with treatment to take total control of my life?

Who am I kidding? How was I going to get through this?

This was my cross to bear and it was as heavy as if someone had dropped a boulder on my chest. When you encounter a boulder, you need to call in someone who has some power to move it. Many questions, so little time, as the monster inside of me continued to multiply and divide. Killing me physically, mentally and spiritually, lurking and waiting on my demise.

Physically Dying

Aching bones, lose teeth, chocolate skin,
what the hell is happening?
Black fingernails smelling of crusty sores
wondering how much more.
Toxic dripping into my veins hour after hour
waiting to kill cells is enough to drive anyone
insane.
The pain of sores in my mouth has cause
Me to lose weight and look paper thin.
No appetite no relief in sight.
I can't fathom why this journey began.
Trying to hold on when I have every reason to let
go.

The first official day of chemotherapy was a dreadful nightmare that I prayed I would wake up from. My mom accompanied me to chemo because she was afraid I wouldn't show up. My support team and I named my treatment "The Terminator." Week after week, I found myself sitting in the "Terminator's chair" wondering if it would be for the last time. I was sitting in horror as I could feel the cells dying inside of me and taking with them the ones that were supposed to protect me. Pushing me to the brink of death with a fever of 103 degrees and my white cell count low.

Doc said, "No chemo today."

But my oncologist overrode that decision and pushed me through. My life was on the line, but at that moment, completing the cycle was more important.

I had to endure five months of chemotherapy. The last two months, I received the chemo drug called "RED DEVIL." The name alone wreaked havoc in every cell, tissue, and fiber of my being. It was like being hit by an 18-wheeler week after week and left to die a slow death. As the toxins set in, the best word that comes to mind is *"Decay."* My body felt like it was decomposing while I was still alive.

Breast surgery for me was as if I was being sliced, diced and gutted like a fish with the scars of a *warrior* in the battle of her life. The night before surgery, I was restless and filled with anxiety. I wanted this to be over and in the same breath wishing it never started. As I pulled up to the hospital, I became weak at the knees but strutted like an ice skater who had just finished a flawless routine and received all tens. I realize I had to fake it until I made it, besides I didn't want my support system to sense anything was wrong. I decided to set the tone for that day. The tone was filled with love, support, anticipation, relief, and faith that God would have the last say so. Surgery was scheduled to start at 6 am but didn't happen until 2 pm because the patient before me ran into complications. We held hands for prayer before surgery, and it was out of our hands. When I woke up in recovery, I was surrounded by *team warriors*; this was the name given to my support system.

The radiation was burning me from the inside out and had me feeling like a lab rat on a cold table, melting away a piece of me with every treatment. I complained to my oncologist about the dramatic changes and her reply was "It's all cosmetics. Everything will return to normal after treatment." The thing was, we both had a *different definition* of what normal was.

After cancer, there is a "new normal," and it's different for each individual. Many look in the mirror and don't recognize the person looking back at them. The entire body is a stranger waiting to become acquainted with the new you. Intimacy can be a horrific experience if you don't have someone who understands, loves, and chooses to be included in the process. You will need someone who is patient with you and can sympathize with you. Accepting the aftermath, the storm leaves behind is a humbling experience. There's no hiding behind beauty or material things. I had to look inside of myself to salvage what was left after the storm. The moment seemed surreal as I attempted to unravel the mystery that was growing inside of me.

I never thought I had the strength to get through something as life-altering as breast cancer. I had to relinquish myself and depend on God to pull me through. God put me in a position where I had to trust in him and him alone. Learning the true meaning of "Let go and let God," is "easier said than done," but possible. I felt like giving up so many times as my body was constantly fatigued and at times unrecognizable. Not to mention the many side effects lurking and seizing any opportunity to knock me off my square.

Neuropathy is one of the side effects that haunt some patients long after treatment is over. Cancer Treatment Centers of America describes neuropathy as "Typically developing in the feet, legs, arms and hands, peripheral neuropathy may be caused by a number of cancer treatments, including radiation therapy and certain chemotherapy drugs. Tumors that press on nerves can also cause peripheral neuropathy, which occurs when peripheral nerves send disruptive sensations to the area of the brain that controls limb movement."[1]

Signs of peripheral neuropathy vary, depending on the nerves involved. Symptoms include:

> Numbness
> Shooting or stabbing pain
> Burning
> Tingling
> Muscle weakness
> Balance disruptions

Loss of fine-motor skills
Difficulty picking up small objects
Constant or random pain
Sensitivity to cold or heat
Limited reflexes
Lack of mobility

This is my reality of dealing with the aftermath of cancer. When neuropathy hits me I just grin and bear it. I try not to highlight it or allow it to disrupt my day-to-day routine.

The impact on my life forced me to get up and live every day "on purpose with purpose." I was not allowed to sit on the sidelines and watch everyone else. I had to get physical. I admit it paralyzed me temporarily and erased my outer beauty, only to replace it with a canvas waiting for the artist to create a better version of me. It took me out of my "comfort zone" and put me "in a zone." I was forced to create my own reality of sexy. I can never get back the old body I was so used to and I'm not sure I would recognize her if I did.

My family rallied around me as they showered me with love and support and cheered me on every step of the way. I admit, I was blessed with an amazing, compassionate hands-on support system. They were there for chemotherapy, surgery and radiation. When I didn't have an appetite, my family, church family and close friends made sure I had everything I needed to get me through. My support system kept me grounded and this really helped contribute to my staying on track and gaining my strength back.

Dying inside physically gave me a chance to appreciate and reflect on the old while admiring the new.

Mentally Dying

I can't fathom why this journey began.
Trying to hold on when I have every reason to let go.
Seeing those little eyes looking up at me
brings me to my knees praying and
asking my heavenly Father to preserve me.
Growing old, wanting to see my seeds in bloom.
Popping pills, hoping to eliminate the residue.
Finding strength I never knew.
Life goes on until the good Lord sees fit.

When we hear someone has cancer, many of us think about the physical aspects. The mental aspect is normally overlooked because it is less visual. The *residue* from cancer lasts years after treatment is long over.

My will to live was constantly tested and the never-ending questions and accusations consumed me!

You're not going to make it!

Your sister died nine months after finding her lump.

Just about everyone you know NEVER wins this battle.

If you take your life now cancer won't stand a chance to take you out.

You were beautiful, but cancer took your hair, your smile, and your confidence, and it will take your life.

You don't stand a chance!

Give up! Give in! No one will blame you!

You read the stats, the Internet reported nine out of ten people who use chemo die. Not to mention the side effects from the toxins, residue, and collateral damage that follow treatment.

You will forever be on edge with aches and pain, wondering if this monster has returned. Besides, God is punishing you and you won't survive.

> *SHUT UP!* I had to tell myself to quite the fears in my mind. *PULL IT TOGETHER!* I had to

make up my mind if I want to attack back. I would not sit idly by while it devours me but I will put on my battle gear and fight until I don't have any fight in me.

Where is GOD?

Why won't He just heal me without my having to go through any of the horrific treatments?

Is God intentionally ignoring me?

You've got my attention, God, now what?

My mind was constantly racing, wondering, and worrying. There is a saying, "If you pray, don't worry...if you're going to worry, why pray?"

Which of you by taking thought can add one cubit unto his stature? (Matthew 6:27 KJV)

My answer is no, but try telling this to my mind, which was in overdrive thinking of all the scenarios of how cancer was going to take me out. It was, at the time, quite unsettling. I was dying inside while still alive as my mind created a hollow grave attempting to swallow me whole. I tried to live my life free from fear, but it was so hard when the devil was in my ear.

Think positive!

That's what everyone says. When did "being positive" take cancer away? I was so sick of feeling paranoid, insane and ashamed. I hid within me and took the blame. Praying, hoping my healing came before they took me away in a strait jacket.

Many recovering from cancer treatment do not take the proper time to heal their mind. Most of us spend years in treatment only to come out battered, bruised, and scarred from the inside out. Yet, somehow, we forget to take a mental break to reflect, get rid of residue, and recharge ourselves. You owe it to yourself to mourn the old you that has passed on with the toxins that were flushed out with treatment.

You will have days where you will experience the stages of grief. Each person experiences the stages differently. There is no right or wrong way to grieve and say goodbye to the old you. According to the Cancer Treatment Centers of America, "cancer may bring on a range of emotions," including, but not limited to, the following:

Shock/disbelief

Fear/uncertainty

Guilt

Grief/sadness

Anxiety

Depression

Anger/frustration

Feelings of isolation

Vulnerability/helplessness

The American Cancer Society also reports, "While it is completely normal to experience any of these emotions during your cancer journey, it does not mean these feelings should be overlooked. It is important to keep your doctor informed about how you are feeling on all levels so he/she can better manage your care." [2]

I can honestly say I've experienced all of these—the full range of emotions—and some at the same time. The initial cancer diagnosis will have you in a dream state, shocked beyond belief and paralyzed, but only for a moment in time.

I have experienced what doctors call "chemo brain." According to The American Cancer Society, "Doctors and researchers call chemo brain many things, such as cancer treatment-related cognitive impairment, cancer-therapy associated cognitive change, or post-chemotherapy cognitive impairment. Most define it as a decrease in mental 'sharpness' being unable to remember certain things and having trouble finishing tasks or learning new skills."[3]

I can recall having a conversation, and in the midst of trying to make a point, my mind would "space out" or I would have a "memory lapse." I wasn't able to remember the point I was about to make. I would play it off by changing the conversation or by pretending to be distracted by something.

On any given day, chemo brain affects those in treatment, and beyond, by causing them to be disorganized and to have slowed thinking and processing as well. Chemo brain still plagues me from time to time with no warning, but I never allow it to take away from my everyday routine. I've invested in journals, making a habit of writing things down and using recording devices.

I had to move on. I couldn't reside there. Fear and uncertainty takes its toll and will be with you throughout your life, but it's how you address it that makes the difference. I was terrified because I felt like my body had betrayed me. I didn't want to open up to anyone for fear of looking crazy, not in control and, yes, vulnerable. Being vulnerable meant admitting I was human and needed someone to assist me. I've always been an in-control, take-charge, do-it-myself individual, so this was a hard pill to swallow. Relinquishing control to God and my trusted support system was not easy. Anxiety seeped in and brought along some friends' name depression, anger, guilt and oh yes, isolation.

"Give up, give in!"

Devil, you are a liar and you won't win.

I had to keep telling myself that. I felt guilty because I was in a teetering position that kept me nauseous inside, like being on a constant ride. There may be moments when you don't want to be bothered by anyone, and others may shy away from you because they really don't know what to say or what you expect from them. Not wanting to impose on anyone, there were periods of isolation that only existed in my mind because my support system never left my side. Having the right ones around you to hold you accountable and to let you have a "moment" is priceless. In my mind, I functioned as if the diagnosis wasn't there, but my body soon told me different. This is where my opportunity to increase my faith and take my relationship with God to a new stage began.

Mourning is a path to receiving healing, but the key is: do *NOT* take up residence there. I know this is easier said than done but it's only by the grace of God I didn't go insane. God kept me!

A cancer diagnosis will strip you of your peace. While going through, many get lost in temporary fillers trying to find peace. Many turn to drugs, alcohol, and even sex, trying to mask anxiety. The inner tranquility that we search for can only come from God, but to receive it, you have to relinquish your worries in their entirety.

I attempted to recall everything I was taught growing up in the church about prayer and healing. I replayed all of God's promises I could remember. Questioning God seemed to be taboo. Nevertheless, I wanted to know the plan God had for my life. My favorite bible verses I've recited through difficult times in my life didn't do it for me now. I needed an encounter with God. I expected God to show up and rescue me, so I wouldn't have to carry this cross. I didn't want to hear the daunting questions that continuously replayed in my mind.

Where is your faith?
What if God chooses not to heal me?
Was my faith game not as strong as I led on?
How can I understand this?

I couldn't even think straight and trying to interpret scripture was not something I had a desire to do. But I wanted God to heal me.

Trust in the Lord with all thy heart; and lean not unto thine own understanding. In all thy ways acknowledge him, and he shall direct thy paths. (Proverbs 3:5-6 KJV)

I've quoted this countless time, but never fully understood its meaning. This was something I couldn't understand on my own. How was I to trust God now? How do I know God hears me? Maybe, after all these years, I really didn't have a connection with God. Was my relationship with God built on religion or was it genuine? Either way, I felt so far from God that I could hear my mom's voice sing, "I looked down the road and I wonder, and I saw how far I was from God." [4]

I began to feel abandoned by God. I wanted to feel Him near me. I expected Him to rescue His daughter. I expected Him to be concerned about me and to repair that which was broken. I was at a point in my life where I didn't feel God's presence, or at least that's how it felt.

I wondered what God's plan was.
What glory can come from my suffering?
What was the beauty in my dying inside?
Was there a purpose for my pain?
How did I find myself in this position?
And what was I being positioned for? Only God knows!

My Pastor, Michael Richardson, of Emanuel COGIC, selected our theme for the year, "Embracing God's Plan: Peace, Progress, and Prosperity."

"For I know the thoughts that I think toward you," saith the Lord, *"thoughts of peace, and not of evil, to give you an expected end." (Jeremiah 29:11 KJV).*

We would all like a sneak peek into God's plan for our lives. Living in peace can be a reality for me if I only relinquish this monster to the one who cares for me. Everything else will fall in place the faster I realize I'm not alone in this fight. There comes a time in your life where you will not know why but will just have to trust God and know He has a plan for your life. This plan is not to bring you to your demise, but to bring glory to Him.

I had a battle to prepare for and cancer wasn't fighting fair. At this point, I decided to bring in some power that could help me pull down the stronghold that was attacking me physically, mentally and spiritually.

Is anything too hard for the Lord? At the time appointed I will return unto thee, according to the time of life, and Sarah shall have a son. (Genesis 18:14 KJV)

God gave Sarah a baby in her 90s; surely, He could heal me of cancer and make me whole again. God delivered Daniel out of the lion's den; cancer didn't stand a chance. God allowed the three Hebrew boys, Shadrach, Meshach and

Abednego, to escape from the fiery furnace unharmed; cancer was no match for an all-powerful God.

<u>BATTLE GEAR</u>

When fighting a battle, you need to make sure you have on the proper gear. The mind has to be at a place where it can stay focused and make decisions without hesitation or distractions. The body has to be in shape so that it can withstand the impact of the enemy. Always include God in your battle and allow Him to lead the way.

His Word instructs us on how to prepare for battle by putting on the whole armor of God:

Put on the whole armor of God, that ye may be able to stand against the wiles of the devil. For we wrestle not against flesh and blood, but against principalities, against powers, against the rulers of the darkness of this world, against spiritual wickedness in high places. Wherefore take unto you the whole armor of God, that ye may be able to withstand in the evil day,

*and having done all, to stand. Stand
therefore, having your loins girt about
with truth, and having on the
breastplate of righteousness; And
your feet shod with the preparation of
the gospel of peace; Above all, taking
the shield of faith, wherewith ye shall
be able to quench all the fiery darts of
the wicked. And take the helmet of
salvation, and the sword of the Spirit,
which is the word of God: Praying
always with all prayer and
supplication in the Spirit, and
watching thereunto with all
perseverance and supplication for all
saints; (Ephesians 6:11-18 KJV)*

When you enter a battle equipped with all
you need to win, your attitude changes, your
posture changes, and your outcome changes. The
person going into battle is not the same person
coming out and the old you has passed away.
There was something different about this battle.
God was stripping me of the *old me* just as the
chemo destroyed the cancer cells. The cells had to
die in order for new ones to grow and properly
divide leaving me free of cancer.

Dying inside was preparation to birth new life in me. I was destined to die inside in order to get in position to bring glory to God. Something new was growing and glowing inside of me. I was no longer dying inside, but was anticipating new life. How could this be? How could I die inside, become pregnant and positioned for purpose? A new birth was forming inside of me and I had found my reason to live.

This storm fueled the passion within.
No longer standing by instead soaring with wings of a warrior.
Trusting, depending and believing in my creator to pull me through.
Knowing there is a rainbow after every storm.
My dawn is near.
Total healing, I pray for,
Physically, mentally, and spiritually.
Leaving me free and empty for my Creator to use me as He pleases.
Total healing is what was granted to thee.

---

1. Cancer Center Treatment of America (n.d.). Peripheral Neuropathy. Retrieved March 26,2018, Retrieved from

https://www.cancercenter.com/ctca-difference/integrative-cancer-treatment/peripheral-neuropathy/

2. Mind-Body Medicine. (2017, July). *Cancer Center Newsletter.* Retrieved March 25, 2018, Retrieved from https://www.cancercenter.com/community/newsletter/july-2007/

3. American Cancer Society (n.d.). Chemo Brain. Retrieved March 25, 2018, Retrieved from https://www.cancer.org/treatment/treatments-and-side-effects/physical-side-effects/changes-in-mood-or-thinking/chemo-brain.html

4. Tharpe, Sister Rosetta. (1947). How Far From God. [Recorded by Tharpe, Sister Rosetta & Price Trio, Sam. New York, NY: Decca.

Chapter 4
Reason to Live

*As I sit in awe of Your love for me, often
wondering
why I came to be.
Am I walking in my God-ordained destiny?
You see, I didn't choose this journey; it chose me
It pursued me, silenced me, and ultimately
qualified me.*

*Cancer attempted to rob me mentally.
I was dying inside not wanting anyone to see into
me.
Stripping my memory of God's promises.
Undermining my cells created to heal me,
it was the trick of the adversary.*

*Walking in your destiny is never easy.
My heavenly father has equipped me, certified me,
justified me,
and set me apart using me as He pleases.*

*Knowing prayer is the key to bring me to my knees,
to unlock sweet victory
as part of His master plan.*

Finding strength to conquer the fears within me.
Trying to sabotage my trust in the Almighty.
Fear attempting to rob me of my inner peace.

History trying to repeat itself,
stopped it in its tracks.
While I take my life back,
keeping my sanity, and minimizing the vanity

Giving thanks to the one who created me,
Father, The Almighty.

Little eyes penetrating my soul and breathing life
into me.
Pleading with me to be strong, hold on never to
give in.

With God it's a guaranteed win.
I've found my second wind,
my reason to live and
no longer living to die
only dying to live.

There's a saying "pregnancy brings a woman closest to death during the birthing experience." Sometimes in life we are put in life or death situations and the old has to die before something new is born.

When a woman becomes pregnant with new life, it is celebrated as a life-changing event. Her appearance takes on a new identity as she begins to add on weight. Some may even say her "skin is glowing and her mane is flowing." Mornings are not always kind to her because they often lead to feelings of nausea, vomiting, fatigue, and increased urination as well as swollen feet.

In the midst of all the commotion the baby's room is being decorated, the name selected, and time is spent picking out a car seat. The body is preparing for new life to pass through the birthing portal. If she's experiencing a bloody show, the baby's head dropping, and contractions, the baby will be arriving soon. The doctor has to make sure she's not experiencing false labor pains.

The last thing a woman wants to do is have the baby before it has a chance to develop. Running into complications can be life threatening for the mom and baby leading to premature birth. Many women grow tired during the nine months and are eager to push before it's time. Some may abort the mission before it has a chance to develop. There are woman who will risk everything to have a safe delivery and healthy baby. The key is to not grow weary or interfere with the developmental stages.

There will be contractions followed by distractions to get your mind off of the miracle that's about to take place. If she can just push past her pain and focus on the outcome, everything will be fine. The birthing experience is one of the most painful parts of bringing new life into the world. When it is time for the baby to come the mother is purposely positioned in a way that will lead to the least amount of pain and discomfort and to a successful outcome for both mommy and baby.

Prior to being told I had cancer, I was diagnosed with blood clots in each lung and prescribed blood thinners. I was instructed while on blood thinners not to get pregnant because the medicine I was prescribed causes skeletal deformities. I found out I was pregnant and immediately became concerned.

I met with my doctor, who told me I had two options. I could have the baby or terminate my pregnancy. I left the doctor's office with a decision to make. I had to decide if I wanted to abort the baby and not have to worry about taking care of a special needs child.

My doctor made it seem like it was the right thing to do, but in the same breath told me, "I'm not giving you permission to terminate. The ultimate decision is yours to make, but do think about the long-term care of the child."

Afraid, and not wanting to deal with what was coming as a result of this unplanned pregnancy, I made an appointment to terminate my baby. This was going to be too much for me to handle and it wasn't fair to bring a baby into the world knowing what type of life it could possibly have. The night before my doctor's appointment I had a dream of my sister Nancy who had passed from breast cancer. There stood a baby in the middle of us as we played tug-of-war.

All I kept hearing her say was, "I don't want this baby," and I was pushing the baby toward her saying the same thing. When I woke up, I decided not to go to the appointment. I made up my mind to go forth with the pregnancy regardless of the outcome. I told myself if this is God's will, let it be. I was helpless, but trusted that God wouldn't put more on me than I could bear.

In May of 2012, I gave birth to a healthy baby girl with no deformities or skeletal issues. I call her my "Miracle Baby."

When you are going through the storms of life, stop, take a deep breath, pray, and ask God for direction. I mean, really seek after Him and wait to hear from Him. Read His Word. How else are you going to know what His will is for your life? You have to read, study and apply His Word to your life. Be still and listen! Communicating in a relationship is a two-way street. Be open to the many different ways God could respond to you.

Breaking News

Little eyes penetrating my soul
Breathing life into me.
Pleading with me to be strong, hold on
never to give in.
With God it's a guaranteed win.
I've found my second wind.
My reason to live.
No longer living to die
only dying to live.

I often think about what my world would look like if I had kept that appointment that day. I'm glad I didn't. What if I had given up because of some news my doctor told me? What if I had given in to my fears? I'm truly grateful for the dream and that I didn't give in. And, I know I'm not alone when I say I wanted to give up. These situations will cause us to want to abort our dreams or purpose before it can be realized. But, if you just hang in there, you will be able to see past the short-term and focus on the long-term outcome while trusting God to direct your path.

I attempted to replay my life out in my head to determine how I arrived at this destination I didn't subscribe too. I came to the conclusion this was payback and God was punishing me for sins I had committed. I tried not to allow fear to paralyze me. I knew I had to take action if I was going to have any chance to survive this horrific disease that has wiped out so many courageous individuals.

I came to grips with my diagnosis. I prepared for war. As a newly single mother of five beautiful children ranging from ages 20 years to 18 months, I had to break the news that Mommy was about to experience a life or death situation and I needed them to brace themselves. This battle was not mine, but God was using me. I needed to show them the fighter in me winning this battle. My biggest fear was revealing my diagnosis to my children. I decided to tell them at different times. Because of the age gaps, I wanted the explanation of my diagnosis to be age appropriate.

I can recall my oldest daughter being by my side when the doctor confirmed the cancer diagnosis. She looked at me wondering what was wrong. I didn't hide it. I told her right away, not knowing what the news would do to her world. She faced her own battles and held them in thinking she had to be strong for me. Her "Warrior" is what she calls me. From the moment she found out, she has been my rock, my prayer warrior, and one of my reasons to live. I wanted her to see me in this real-life situation and know I was a fighter and didn't give up.

I cringed at the thought of my girls having to worry about breast cancer in their future. Cancer shouldn't be a lifelong diagnosis. At some point, I should be able to walk away and never look back.

My son was on leave from the military for Christmas break, and this was my opportunity to share my news with him. I asked him to take a ride with me. I pulled over and dropped the bomb on him. As a man, he was compassionate, but hid his true feelings from me in order to remain strong for the girls and me. He has been by my side even though he was stationed in another country. He was there for my surgery and took care of me afterwards. I didn't want to disappoint him; he believed in his mother. He was my strength when I didn't want to be strong. He's definitely helped me find a reason to live.

I intentionally didn't immediately share my news with my three little ones due to fear it might be devastating enough to affect them mentally. I didn't want them to see my bald head or even see me shed a tear. Not that it wasn't okay to cry, but I didn't want them to be so focused on the physical that they couldn't see past it. I wanted them to always remember a version of me with strength and hope, that even though you go through you don't have to look like you are caught in a storm.

However, I did want them to know this diagnosis was real. Once I broke the news to them, I sent them to visit their father for the summer, so I could complete chemotherapy and not have to worry about being too weak to care for them.

Sending the girls to Vegas to stay with their dad was so hard for me. They were always with me and I felt so alone without them in the house. As long as they were there I felt useful, like someone needed me. Simple tasks like taking my girls to school became a major event that took every ounce of energy in me. I felt like I was losing my health and now my family and possibly my life.

I felt defeated!

How did I allow this to happen?

How could I let my babies down?

How could I?

I wasn't ready to expose them to every aspect of my diagnosis. I didn't want to contaminate their memory of me if I didn't make it. I didn't want their last memories of me to be a bald head and frail frame. You know, the poster child for anyone who has cancer. I didn't want them to make that connection, but they eventually did because they are very inquisitive girls.

I've found not one, not two, but five reasons to live. When I can't fight for myself, I have five reasons that forced me to continue to show up to fight. I wanted to see my seeds bloom, and their seeds, and so on. I didn't want to miss the milestones like proms, graduations, my son getting married, and my glam baby. Watching my daughters growing up and becoming young women. I wanted to help my baby girl move into her college dorm.

I decided I wanted and needed to be here for all the bumps, bruises, heartbreaks, and celebrations. Being a single parent was hard enough; I didn't want them to have to worry about who was going to take care of them. I was the head of household and if I didn't work we wouldn't eat or have a place to lay our heads. This caused me to push forward through treatment with the least amount of downtime.

Once all five of my children were on the same page I didn't have to hide my bald head anymore. I was free to go through this journey without feeling guilty or like I had let them down. They were really up-close-and-personal for the duration of my journey. They encouraged me to fight my best fight and rest when I needed to rest, often stepping in to lend a hand with household chores, and even going to treatment with me. They took part in breast cancer events at school on my behalf to show solidarity. Just being able to see their little faces and hear the word "mommy" each day was healing for me and my ultimate reason to live.

My encounter with God

As I sit in awe of Your love for me, often wondering
why I came to be.
Am I walking in my God-ordained destiny?
You see, I didn't choose this journey; it chose me
It pursued me, silenced me and ultimately qualified me.

My relationship with God had to go to another level in order for me to get through this. I admit I wasn't seeking God with passion before because I was satisfied with just saying I knew him. The real test came when I had to go beyond the surface of my relationship with God. Just like any other relationship you have to nurture it, or it will not blossom. I had to spend time with God in order to increase intimacy. If you don't put in the work or quality time, then you are wasting precious time that you will never recover.

I had to start off by getting to know God. Sometimes we think we know a person and we really haven't taken the time to invest in the relationship. My thirst for God grew. I began seeking God intensity, wanting and needing to commune with Him.

There is healing in the Blood

Cancer attempted to rob me mentally.
I was dying inside not wanting anyone to see into me.
Stripping my memory of God promises.
Undermining my cells created to heal me,
it was the trick of the adversary.

Memorial Day weekend in 2014 I wasn't able to stand up for more than a minute without wiping out. I got exhausted attempting simple tasks like getting dressed. I assumed it was one of the side effects from chemo. Nothing I did, and no amount of rest, satisfied how fatigued I was.

On top of that I had a fever that wouldn't go down. I had been dealing with this all day, so I was just going to sleep it off, but I wasn't able to sleep. It was midnight. I put on some inspirational music as I lay in bed, but I couldn't get comfortable because I was in so much pain.

I got on my knees and prayed and cried saying, "Lord, Lord, Lord, I need a word from you. I needed to know I'm going to be okay."

I read all of my healing scriptures. I read God's promises back to Him with anticipation of His keeping His Word. I needed God to move and I needed Him to move now.

I laid prostrate on my bed and again called out, "Lord, Lord, Lord, I need a word from You. I needed to know I'm going to be okay."

All of a sudden, the atmosphere of the room changed. The song playing on the radio was by Byron Cage, *The Presence of the Lord Is Here*! I immediately wiped my tears and sat up. I acknowledge my Lord and thanked Him for what He'd already done. I thanked Him for hearing my cry and proceeded to tell Him what I desired from Him.

"Lord, preserve me, heal me, allow me to see my children's children grow up and old, and use me for your glory."

The next song that came on the radio was by DeWayne Woods, *Let Go.* [5]

Couldn't seem to fall asleep
There was so much on my mind
Searching for that peace
But the peace I could not find
So then I knelt down to pray
Praying help me please
Then He said you don't have to cry
'Cause I'll supply all your needs
As soon as I stop worrying
Worrying how the story ends
I let go and I let God
Let God have His way

Letting go was very hard for me. I was out of my comfort zone. I felt unbalanced when I had to depend on someone else but this time it was different, because it was my Lord.

I knew at that moment I had an encounter with God. I was in awe of my Lord for coming to see about me. I can't even describe the peace that came over me when I felt His presence in the room. I was able to sleep because I knew my joy was coming in the morning. On this night, I received my peace that surpasses all understanding.

7 And the peace of God, which passeth all understanding, shall keep your hearts and minds through Christ Jesus. (Philippians 4:7 KJV).

It wasn't over. The next day, I was still in pain. I asked my mom to cook me some of her famous tomato beef soup. She prepared it and came over to serve it to me. Who doesn't love their mom's cooking? It always seems to make anything better. The soup didn't do it for me, and that's when I knew I better contact my doctor and find out what was really going on. I was instructed to go to the emergency room. I was more worried about the big pot of soup I left behind going to waste.

Upon arrival to the emergency room, I was told my blood was very low and I needed a blood transfusion. I was admitted, and the procedure started soon after. The very thought of someone else's blood being pumped into my veins made me sick to my stomach, but there was no other way.

God knows how to get my attention. I didn't have a charger for my phone because I was so focused on my pain I didn't bring it, plus I didn't think I was going to be admitted. God took my mind off of it by sending me an angel to sit and talk to me the entire time the transfusion was taking place. She had been with me from the beginning and knew firsthand what I was going through.

As the blood was being pumped into my veins, her phone rang and she handed it to me. It was my pastor checking in on me. He closed out our conversation with a prayer. The only thing that came to mind was a saying I've heard too many times, "There is healing in the blood." I truly understood what it meant because I instantly felt like a new woman. Thank you, JESUS, for the blood. It indeed gave me strength.

Is anyone among you sick? Let him call for the elders of the church, and let them pray over him,

*anointing him with oil in the name of the Lord.
And the prayer of faith will save the sick, and the
Lord will raise him up. And if he has committed
sins, he will be forgiven (James 5:14-15 KJV).*

God communicated with me in a vision that
showed me in the future. He showed me exactly
what I would be doing and how I would look. I
was standing in front of a room filled with women
as if I was teaching or giving a speech. My hair
was neatly cut short and I had a skirt that came to
my knees and a flowered blouse. I could tell the
women were enjoying whatever I was saying
because of their postures and facial expressions. At
this very moment, I knew God was going to heal
me. He allowed me to see myself outside of my
sickness. I didn't tell anyone right away what I saw
because it kind of frightened me. It was blowing
my mind that God was even communicating with
me.

I mean, I've heard the stories from other
people before but had never experienced it for
myself. This was my defining moment. This was
the beginning of life and love for self. When I
made the decision to take my focus off of dying
inside and put my energy towards my reason to

live was when my reason for going through this storm became clearer to me. It was not about me; it was never about me.

My work here on earth was not finished. I had barely touched the surface of operating in my new-found purpose. I didn't make the connection that my breast cancer diagnosis was positioning me for purpose. God had to be able to trust me with the test that I would take the lesson and share it while recognizing the blessing.

The rest was up to me, to set the wheels in motion. I have a newfound appreciation for life. I appreciate everything about it and my relationship with God. It was also at this point that I claimed my healing even before my treatment had ended or surgery was performed. I had made up in my mind that my healing was granted to me the moment God revealed me in the future. This fueled a fire in me, and I decided to work to decrease or eliminate the number of women and men who experience cancer altogether. I wasn't going to sit idly by and watch others go through what I went through.

I made it my mission to reach back and be that voice for patients before, during, and after a cancer diagnosis. I encourage all of them to move "away from awareness toward action."

As I look back, I think about all the times I wanted to give up and give in to my fears. All of the distractions that were thrown at me to get me off course. The attacks on me physically, mentally and spiritually had the potential to rob me of my future. Staying focused and aware of what I need to do in order to survive was crucial. Dying inside is a silent killer because no one can physically see the process happening. As soon as you make up in your mind to "let go and let God" you've already won.

This journey had so many meanings. I believe it was to bring me closer to God, to bring others closer to Him by sharing my testimony, and to serve others who are in need of this lifesaving information. I also believe my relationship with God kept me focused on the bigger picture. I'm grateful God thought enough of me to honor my request and came to see about me. I am thankful that the distractions that came upon me didn't pull me back into a life without God. Finding my reason to live didn't come easy, but it gave me a newfound appreciation for the people in my life and for the meaning of life. Learning not to take time for granted because once it's gone we can't get a refund. I've learned to always be ready because we never know what God has in store for us. The storm doesn't always come to kill you. Sometimes the storm comes to qualify you while positioning you for a purpose that will bring glory and honor to God.

Position and Prepare

Walking in your destiny is never easy.
My heavenly father has equipped me, certified me,
justified me,
and set me apart
using me as he please.
Knowing prayer is the key to bring me to my knees.
Unlocking sweet victory
as part of his master plan.
Finding strength to conquer the fears within me.

When the storm you're going through seems as if it's consuming you, PRESS. When it feels like you are being swallowed up by a black hole and you can't see the light of day, PRESS. Even when you feel like everything inside and around you are dying, PRESS. The PRESSure of the storm is preparing to propel you into the plan God has for your life that will ultimately bring glory to Him.

I came to the conclusion that everything I've endured up until now was a culmination of God positioning me for His purpose. My encounter with God was bigger than my encounter with fear. It gave me the fuel that I needed to *PRESS FORWARD.* This allowed me a sneak peek into the plan God has for my life and gave me the fuel I needed to *PRESS FORWARD.* Make a decision that on a daily basis you will stop LIVING TO DIE, but instead you will make every effort to DIE TO LIVE. In life we will have trials and tribulations. The key is prayer and preparation in advance for what's to come.

5, 4, 3, 2, 1…

According to statistics, you are not considered a survivor until you have *five years* of being cancer free. The doctors will only recognize you as being in remission or no EOD (evidence of disease). Whenever someone asks me if I am in remission I tell them, "NO, I'M HEALED."

According to the Oxford Dictionary, remission is defined as, "A temporary diminution of the severity of disease or pain." [6]

When someone is healed, they are not thinking on temporary terms. According to Merriam-Webster Dictionary, healing is defined as, *to make free from injury or disease: to make sound or whole heal a wound...to restore to original purity or integrity.* [7]

I am entering my *fifth year* of being healed in 2018 and all glory goes to God. I have been operating in my non-for-profit for *four years* as an advocate and ambassador, spreading the importance of early detection, knowing your risks in order to reduce them, knowing your family history, and making healthier lifestyle choices.

Warriors Talk, Inc. NFP Est. 2014 was birthed out of my cancer journey. I began sharing my testimony on how God healed me and is using me to empower individuals into this *movement of action.*

After brainstorming with a friend about the possibilities of hosting a radio show on an unrelated topic, it just didn't seem to be working out. All talks ended up focusing on cancer education, awareness, and action. In October 2015 an opportunity came along for me to host my own radio broadcast. I needed a platform where I could educate and empower individuals into action on a consistent basis. Now, keep in mind this was not something I planned to do before my diagnosis. I've always considered myself as a very shy and behind-the-scenes type of person, so this was definitely out of my comfort zone. I found myself being asked to be a speaker and to facilitate workshops around the Chicago metropolitan area.

The *Warriors Talk* Radio Broadcast is going on *three years* old. The platform is to address how cancer as well as other diseases are running rampant throughout our country and how we can move away from awareness toward taking action. We keep listeners informed and connected to services as we encourage them to thrive while surviving. The *Warriors Talk* Radio Broadcast also allows survivors an opportunity to share their journey with individuals before, during, and after a cancer diagnosis.

October 2017 marked the *second year* for the "Survivors Night of Reflection Gala." This event gives survivors an opportunity to reflect on their journey and how they are grateful to be here to share their experience, knowledge, and wisdom on conquering cancer. This night is our annual fundraiser for those currently in battle. Funds raised go to our *Warriors in the Battle Fund*. This fund is available to individuals in the midst of fighting cancer and need some financial assistance to bridge the gap financially so that they are able to concentrate on fighting and healing. A portion of the funds is also used for *Battle Buddy Sacs.* These sacks are put together with items handpicked and distributed to cancer centers throughout the Chicago metropolitan area and surrounding suburbs. The sacs contain items to relax the mind, reduce stress, calm fears, and document their journey while keeping their minds on thriving and surviving.

I am grateful to be alive to share my journey as a first-time author. I'm a witness, just *one* encounter with God can change the course of your journey.

5 Morton, Paul Jr. & Woods, DeWayne. (2006). Let Go. Airbourne Audio, Lenaxa, KS:Verity.

6 https://en.oxforddictionaries.com/definition/remission

7 https://www.merriam-webster.com/dictionary/heal

HEALING SCRIPTURES

*All Scripture quotations, unless otherwise
indicated, are taken from the
King James Version.*

Proverbs 3:5-6
*5 Trust in the Lord with all thine heart; and lean
not unto thine own understanding
6 In all thy ways acknowledge him, and he shall
direct thy paths.*

James 5:14-15
*14 Is anyone among you sick? Let him call for the
elders of the church, and let them pray over him,
anointing him with oil in the name of the Lord. 15
And the prayer of faith will save the sick, and the
Lord will raise him up. And if he has committed
sins, he will be forgiven.*

Jeremiah 29:11
*11 For I know the thoughts that I think toward you,
saith the Lord, thoughts of peace, and not of evil,
to give you an expected end.*

1 Peter 5:7
*7 Casting all your care upon him; for he careth for
you.*

Philippians 4:7
7 And the peace of God, which passeth all understanding, shall keep your hearts and minds through Christ Jesus.

Matthew 6:27
27 Which of you by taking thought can add one cubit unto his stature?

Genesis 18:14
14 Is anything too hard for the Lord? At the time appointed I will return unto thee, according to the time of life, and Sarah shall have a son.

Ephesians 6:11-18
11 Put on the whole armor of God, that ye may be able to stand against the wiles of the devil.
12 For we wrestle not against flesh and blood, but against principalities, against powers, against the rulers of the darkness of this world, against spiritual wickedness in high places.
13 Wherefore take unto you the whole armor of God, that ye may be able to withstand in the evil day, and having done all, to stand.
14 Stand therefore, having your loins girt about with truth, and having on the breastplate of righteousness;

15 And your feet shod with the preparation of the gospel of peace;
16 Above all, taking the shield of faith, wherewith ye shall be able to quench all the fiery darts of the wicked.
17 And take the helmet of salvation, and the sword of the Spirit, which is the word of God:
18 Praying always with all prayer and supplication in the Spirit, and watching thereunto with all perseverance and supplication for all saints;

Psalm 118:17
7 I shall not die, but live, and declare the works of the Lord.

Psalm 103:1-5
103 Bless the Lord, O my soul: and all that is within me, bless his holy name.
2 Bless the Lord, O my soul, and forget not all his benefits:
3 Who forgiveth all thine iniquities; who healeth all thy diseases;
4 Who redeemeth thy life from destruction; who crowneth thee with lovingkindness and tender mercies;

5 Who satisfieth thy mouth with good things; so that thy youth is renewed like the eagle's.

Joshua 21:45
45 There failed not ought of any good thing which the Lord had spoken unto the house of Israel; all came to pass.

Psalm 91:16
16 With long life will I satisfy him and shew him my salvation.

3 John 2
2 Beloved, I wish above all things that thou mayest prosper and be in health, even as thy soul prospereth.

Isaiah 53:3
3 He is despised and rejected of men; a man of sorrows and acquainted with grief: and we hid as it were our faces from him; he was despised, and we esteemed him not.

Matthew 18:19
19 Again I say unto you, That if two of you shall agree on earth as touching any thing that they

shall ask, it shall be done for them of my Father which is in heaven.

2 Timothy 1:7
7 For God hath not given us the spirit of fear; but of power, and of love, and of a sound mind.

Isaiah 43:2
2 When thou passest through the waters, I will be with thee; and through the rivers, they shall not overflow thee: when thou walkest through the fire, thou shalt not be burned; neither shall the flame kindle upon thee.

Philippians 4:8
8 Finally, brethren, whatsoever things are true, whatsoever things are honest, whatsoever things are just, whatsoever things are pure, whatsoever things are lovely, whatsoever things are of good report; if there be any virtue, and if there be any praise, think on these things.

Revelation 12:11
11 And they overcame him by the blood of the Lamb, and by the word of their testimony; and they loved not their lives unto the death.

Job 5:26
Thou shalt come to thy grave in a full age, like as a
shock of corn cometh in in his season.

Nahum 1:9
What do ye imagine against the Lord? he will
make an utter end: affliction shall not rise up the
second time.

ACKNOWLEDGMENTS

All praises and honor to God for my journey and positioning me for purpose. Thank you to my family, friends and church family that played a role before, during and after my journey. I thank you from the bottom of my heart. I couldn't have made it through the storm without your love, support and encouragement. #**TeamWarriors** #**Warriorstalk1**

<u>STAY CONNECTED</u>
Facebook/warriorstalks
Facebook: warriorstalkw/ladyreshell
Twitter: @warriorstalk1
Instagram: warriorstalk1
Periscope: @warriorstalk1
Email: warriorstalk1@gmail.com
Website: <u>www.warriorstalk.org</u>
Donations: <u>www.paypal.me/warriorstalk1</u>

<u>Meet Lady ReShell Matheny</u>

Lady ReShell Matheny is a stage two breast cancer survivor. She has undergone chemotherapy, surgery and radiation. Being a breast cancer survivor, her mission in life is to empower, encourage and support all those touched by cancer. She is currently a Cancer ambassador. She educates the community on the importance of cancer risks and early detection. She is the founder of Warriors Talk Inc. NFP Est. 2014 where she provides a cancer mentorship radio broadcast that assist women in improving the quality and quantity of life while thriving to survive.

Currently an Education Ambassador for Bright Pink. The mission is to save women lives from breast and ovarian cancer by empowering women to live proactively at a young age.

She was selected and currently serves as a Ford Warrior in Pink Model of Courage. The mission is to provide cancer patient with more good days.

A Community Volunteer Ambassador with the American Cancer Society. She currently educates the community and supports the needs of cancer patients.

She has earned her BA Degree in Criminal Justice at Aurora University in 2003. She currently works as a Probation Officer for the past 14 years where she enjoys changing lives one at a time.

She has earned her MBA with a consecration in Human Resources at Aurora University in 2008. She uses her knowledge to assist her clients with finding substantial employment.

Served as President of Ladies of Nu World Ryders where she performed Outreach from 2007 to 2013 spearheading community service events such as: toys-for-tots, back-to-school and hot plate giveaways.

In her free time she enjoys writing poetry as well as performing on open mic.

She also spends time with her children taking in all the beautiful Chicago attractions.

Lady ReShell
Host | Survivor | Advocate | Ambassador | Speaker | Facilitator

Warriors Talk, Inc. NFP Est. 2014
~Away From Awareness Toward Action

<u>Introducing Stephanie Saintyl</u>

Stephanie Saintyl is an up and coming powerhouse on the Motivational Speaker scene. She once upon a time had to battle with an identity crisis wondering if people were seeing her as she saw herself. If you have not identified who you are, it is easy for you to be identified by others. Many times, our past can make us feel like a "lost puzzle piece" trying to fit in where ever we can instead of the "wonderfully made masterpieces" that GOD created us to be.

Stephanie talks about her journey of self discovery and "self lovery" in these inspirational chapters. She has MOVED from a PAST filled with doubts about who she was and whose she was. Now she no longer worries about how she was perceived , but walks firmly in her PURPOSE of helping Women know themselves and become the C.G.G.A. 's they were created to be! In these chapters, she will provide you with tips to help you too.

Want to know what C.G.G.A. is? Keep reading this truly Unstoppable story of MOVING from PAST to PURPOSE!

~ Terrance Leftridge

Chapter 5
A Lost Puzzle Piece

Have you ever examined the characteristics of a puzzle piece? If you have, you would've noticed that it has a specific shape, color, and size, which allow it to fit perfectly within a puzzle. Each one of us is a piece of the universal puzzle called life. Some of us naturally know where we belong, and then there are some of us who struggle to find our perfect fit. Our personalities, traits, and skills all shape our identities which help us determine where we belong in life. However, what if you are not aware of who you are? Would you still be able to identify where you fit in? Or would you feel like I did five years ago, like a lost puzzle piece that couldn't find its place?

In 2011, I started my first year of college at Eastern Illinois University. Like any other freshman, I was nervous, but I was excited to embark on this new chapter in my life. By my first week I became friends with four other girls who were also freshmen. In less than a month, we became inseparable! We walked around campus together, ate lunch together, studied together, and of course partied together. Now, today, you wouldn't dare catch me at a college party. As I reflect back on my life, I realize that I never really gave any thought to whether or not I even liked to go to parties. I see now that I was just "going along to get along." I never once took the time to ask myself *Do I genuinely like what I am doing, or am I doing it just to fit in?*

The more my friends and I hung out together, the more I got to know them, and they got to know me. Growing up, I was often told that I initially come off as being stuck up. I personally never saw myself as being stuck up, but I did know that I was a very shy and quiet girl. In school I didn't raise my hand to speak in class, nor did I race over to introduce myself to my classmates. Although I was a bit skeptical as to why people had that perception of me, I never explored the reasoning behind it. I mean, if everyone is saying the same thing about you, why question it? It must be true, right? Take a moment right now and reflect back on your own life. I am pretty sure you can recall a time when someone perceived you incorrectly, and you didn't think twice about it.

Since I was already used to being called stuck up, it didn't surprise me when my closest friends gave me the nickname "bougie" in college, which is a slang word for someone who is perceived to be "uppity." I will never forget one night when we sat down in the dorm to discuss weekend plans. Everyone had suggested that we should do something as a group. However, I knew that I couldn't be with them that weekend and without thinking, came right out and said "I won't be with you guys, I have other plans." Before I could finish my sentence, I was already getting the side eye from everyone.

Several days later, I learned that occasionally the other girls in the group felt like I did not care to be around them.... Now put yourself in my shoes for a minute. Your friends, who you actually love being around, have just informed you that everyone else thinks you don't like being with them. Of course, like any other group, we had our ups and downs, but never once did I ever consider that I myself as being a problem. If someone was telling you something that you knew wasn't true, wouldn't you begin to be confused? In my mind, I knew I was one of the quietest girls in the group and I did the same things that everyone else did.

So why do people feel this way about me?

How did Stephanie become the issue?

Back then, I never considered that what I said, or specifically *how* I said things, to my friends was an issue. Neither was I aware of my *unfriendly* facial expressions, and the assertive tone in my voice that drew people away from me.

It was not until I took myself out of the frame that I was able to look at the entire picture. I saw why people had a hard time developing an accurate perception of me. Throughout my life, I had never established my own identity. I didn't have an accurate perception of myself, so how was it possible for others to have a clear understanding of who Stephanie was? The fact that I never took the time to explore who I was made it easy for me to just go with the flow. It was easier to just accept what people thought of me, instead of establishing my own individuality.

However, now I see that if I had truly taken the time to invest in becoming my own person, I would have realized that some things I participated in…just weren't me. Since it was normal to party and drink every weekend in college, I conformed to that lifestyle. Even though I always knew in the back of my mind that this "party life" wasn't for me, I did it anyway. Most of the time, I felt like I had to "fake it" just to have a good time. Every time I went to a party, I was uncomfortable. I felt like a puzzle piece that had been placed in the wrong box. This leads me to my first point in how NOT to become a "Lost Puzzle Piece."

Point #1: Don't conform to the identity others perceive you to have.

Les Brown once said, "Don't let someone else's opinion of you become YOUR reality!" 1 It is very common for us to just go with the flow of everything around us. If everyone dresses a certain way, we dress that same way. If everyone likes a certain show, we start watching that show. If our friends are going out late at night, best believe we are too! We seldom pause and ask ourselves, *Is this even me?*

Maybe right now, you have been conforming to things that you know is out of your character. Next time you think about following the crowd, pause and ask yourself a few questions:

Is my conscious telling me not to do this?

Am I doing this just to fit in?

Will doing this make me feel uncomfortable?

If you answered "yes" to these questions, then I encourage you to STOP what you are doing. When you conform to doings things that are contrary to who you are, you are only confusing yourself and slowing down the journey towards reaching your fullest potential.

Each one of us has our own unique purpose in this puzzle called life. However, if you continue to do what everyone else is doing, you will never discover it. You may not realize it, but every time you do something that is outside of your nature, you are walking away from your destiny, instead of walking towards it. Your destiny is tied to your purpose, and your purpose is tied to your identity. So, make sure you are surrounding yourself with the right pieces to *your* life's puzzle! Not everything you do, and not everyone you're with will lead you to your purpose.

Start walking to the beat of your own drum, instead of conforming to others. If you are like I was, and you never established your own beat, then start hitting a drum until you find a beat you like! Figure out what makes you different and embrace your individuality. If you are a vegan, be proud of that! If you don't drink, be proud of that! If you are a bookworm, be proud of that! If you are celibate, be proud of that!

NEVER compromise who you are just to fit in, and NEVER do something you are not comfortable doing. Remember you are living for yourself, NOT for other people. If you don't fit comfortably within a puzzle, then it's time for you to find a NEW puzzle.

With senior year around the corner, it was evident that not knowing who I was was affecting my future. In my junior year my friends, family, and everyone else you could imagine wanted to know what was *next* for Stephanie? What was Stephanie going to do after she graduated? As a child, I considered being a teacher, a social worker, and a pediatrician. I never established or discovered that *one thing* I was really passionate about, or what I felt I was born to do. I had an idea, but never had my heart set on a specific career.

Therefore, the only answer I could come up with was "I don't know yet...."

That reallyyyy didn't go over well with my parents because their response was, "How are you about to be a senior in college and you don't know what you want to do with your life? We are not paying for your education just for you to not know what you want to do with it!"

I began to question why I didn't know what I wanted to do, while everyone else around me had their lives perfectly mapped out. All of my peers were already applying to graduate schools, starting internships, and talking about how they couldn't wait to graduate and start working in their career field. While I was sitting there trying to figure out what field I should even be in! Could you imagine how I was feeling?

I just couldn't wrap my head around the fact that I went to class like everyone else, I met with my advisor regularly, and I was constantly on the dean's list, yet I didn't have a clear post-graduation plan! I felt like everyone else around me was putting all their puzzle pieces together, but I couldn't even find the pieces that belonged to me. This leads me to my second point…

Point #2: Learn not to compare yourself to the other puzzle pieces in the pile.

You may be at a stage in life where everyone around you is graduating, getting married, starting a business, or having kids…and you're asking yourself, *When is it going to be my turn?* Do me one favor. Take your eyes off of their lives and start to focus on YOUR life! Your life doesn't have to match up with everyone else's in order to be purposeful. You are unique, so your journey will also be unique. Whether you believe it or not, there is something amazing unfolding in your life right now. Stop narrowing your perspective, and start opening your eyes to the endless opportunities right in front of you.

On the other hand, maybe you aren't the one comparing yourself to others, but your family members are. Do me another favor. Don't SETTLE because of the pressure! Don't allow other people in your life to make you feel inadequate or that you need to rush into something. My dad suggested over and over that I pursue a career in the medical field. However, after I shadowed a few medical occupations, I instantly knew that the medical lifestyle was not, and I repeat, was NOT for me. Even though I knew he had good intentions for me, that career field just wasn't the right fit for Stephanie. If I had chosen to settle, I know without a doubt that I would have been miserable at work.

It's like when we are almost done with a 100-piece puzzle. With only a few pieces left, we try to rush the process. We are so ready to experience the finished product that we just start putting pieces anywhere. Then we become aggravated when the pieces don't fit. However, if we had **FIRST** taken our time to examine the puzzle pieces, it would have been clear as to where the pieces fit, and where they don't. Everyone's journey to finding their perfect fit *takes time*. Don't rush it. It's not about how quickly you get to the destination, but about what you learn and experience while on the journey that makes it worthwhile.

These are the things I had only wished I knew in college. At that time, I thought that by doing things other people wanted me to do, everything would just magically fall right into place. However, instead of things falling into place, everything started falling apart. No matter what I tried to do, I found myself moving backward, instead of forward. I became sick and tired of being called "bougie." I got sick and tired of people telling me what I should be doing. I got sick and tired of not knowing what I wanted for my life, and I got sick and tired of watching everyone's life come together, while mine crumbled before my eyes!

By the time I got back to college for my senior year, I found myself at a breaking point. I found myself sitting on my living room floor with tears running down my face, and I began to think about my situation. The more I reflected, the more I realized that I was just confused!

Am I loosing myself?

Am I trying too hard to please other people?

Do I even know how to please myself?

I then asked myself a very simple, but vital question:

What are five things I love about myself?

Now, the typical person would think that you would be able to come up with these five things in a heartbeat; that wasn't the case for me. I found myself looking at the clock, and minutes had gone by, not just seconds. I looked down at my paper, and I realized that I had only come up with three things! How was it that I could ONLY come up with a maximum of three things I loved about myself? Have you ever had a moment in your life where you asked yourself a defining question like that? I challenge you right now to take out a pen and paper and start writing out at least five things that YOU love about yourself.

At that very moment, I determined to start what I call my *Self-Lovery Journey*. "Self-lovery" is a combination of self-love and self-discovery. I knew that in order to become a better me, I had to first know what people thought of me. It was time to finally get the feedback from my friends and loved ones that I had avoided for so long. I asked everyone to tell me:

- What is it about my facial expressions that make people think I am stuck up?
- What is it about the way I speak to people that pushes them away from me?
- What do you like about me?
- What don't you like about me?

I wanted to gather enough information to help me understand how people truly viewed Stephanie.

Once I got the feedback I needed, I was able to clearly put the pieces of the puzzle together to see a clear picture of what other people thought of me. I learned that my "stale face," or the frown I had unintentionally on my face, gave people the impression I didn't want to be bothered. I also discovered that when I spoke to people, I had a very assertive and authoritative tone in my voice that made people feel inferior to me. Although it was hard to hear their feedback, this was my reality. I was determined to use it as motivation to change their perspective of me. I was determined to no longer compare myself to the other puzzle pieces in the box. I was determined to become the best me I could be.

Instead of people seeing me as stuck up, I wanted people to see me as approachable. Instead of pushing people away from me, I wanted to attract the right people to me. Instead of being a follower, I wanted to be a leader. Instead of being selfish, I wanted to be more empathic. Instead of trying to act like someone else, I wanted to proudly embrace my own uniqueness.

To practice exemplifying these characteristics, I made a goal that every week I would do something that represented a specific attribute I wanted to be known for and reflect on the experience of implementing it. As an only child, for example, I had a bad case of "spoiled-brat syndrome." If things didn't go my way, you were sure to know it. At one point, I was so bad that my mom even got tired of my attitude and didn't want to do things for me anymore. I clearly remember the time I complained all day when I found out that I might not be able to get my hair done the exact way I wanted it. Did I mention it was at least $250 to get it done!? Although I did end up getting it done the way I requested, I failed to show my mom that I was appreciative of the financial sacrifice she made just to make me happy. I was determined to show my mom that the old Stephanie had left the building and a new Stephanie was in town!

Before she came home from work one day, I decided to clean the entire house. I washed the dishes, swept the floors, wiped down the furniture, and even organized the closets. I made sure the place was spotless. Even "Mr. Clean" would have been impressed by me! When she walked through the door, her eyes lit up! I will never forget how surprised and grateful she was by my thoughtfulness. She told me that she was very proud of me and could get used to this **NEW** Stephanie. Seeing the smile on my mom's face encouraged me to continue seeking out opportunities to show compassion, empathy, and appreciation towards others.

Within less than three months, my friends and family started seeing a difference in my entire demeanor. To know that they were beginning to see me in a new light motivated me to grow into a better person in every way possible. I made a goal that every month I would read a new self -help book. The very first one I read was called *The Everything Self-Esteem Book,* by Robert M. Sherfield. Now, I can't even lie; I was a bit hesitant to read a book about self-esteem. I just knew that I didn't have self-esteem issues. I started to judge the book by its cover and thought to myself, *Now, how is a book about "self-esteem" going to help me reach my fullest potential?* I thank God I didn't let my judgment prevent me from opening it up.

This book completely transformed the way I viewed myself and other people. It taught me that in order to reach my fullest potential, I needed to be the creator of my own happiness, do things that are outside of my comfort zone and, most importantly, I have to be confident in who I am. Everything I learned from the book, I applied to my life. To further boost my confidence, I started to recite daily affirmations of what type of person I was striving to be.

I am confident in whatever I do.

I enjoy my own company.

I live in the present and not in the past.

I am a joy to be around.

I embrace new opportunities.

I am on the journey toward reaching my fullest potential and no one can stop me. I am **UNSTOPPABLE!**

I challenged myself to be committed to doing something outside of my comfort zone every week. The more I experienced new things, I became enlightened to skills, talents, and abilities that I never knew I had! Before I knew it, I became addicted to stepping outside of my comfort zone and fell in love with reaching my fullest potential. It was when I stopped conforming and comparing myself to others that I started to see my life wasn't falling apart, but piecing itself together in a unique way. I discovered what truly brought joy to my life, the things I couldn't live without, and even what career field I was interested in! I started developing my own hobbies, goals, and standards. Most importantly, I began to fall in love with everything that made me… Stephanie. This brings me to my last point.

Point #3: What makes a puzzle piece the perfect fit? Knowing what type of puzzle piece it is!

"A man who stands for nothing will fall for anything"[2] *(Malcolm X).*

Do you know what makes you laugh? What makes you cry? What your personality is like? Do you know what you like? Do you know what you dislike? What are your values? What are your goals in life? What makes you unique?

*If you don't remember anything from this chapter, remember this:

Only when you know who you are, will you know where you belong.

Maybe you don't know who you are **YET**, and that's okay, because I know who you are. You are **UNIQUE!** The way you dress is unique. The way you talk is unique. The way you walk is unique. Even the way you think is unique! It's time that you start embracing your uniqueness! No one can be a better you than you. So be the best you, you can be!

Don't know where to start? Here are five things you can start doing now!

- Set goals for yourself.
- Recite daily affirmations.
- Do things outside of your comfort zone.
- Surround yourself with positivity.
- Read self-help books.
- Do whatever you have to do to become the BEST you!

It's because I never realized I was unique that I didn't set clear standards for myself. I just went wherever the wind blew. However, once I started putting the right pieces together, I could clearly see that I wasn't a lost puzzle piece, but a wonderfully made masterpiece!

Chapter 6

A Wonderfully Made Masterpiece

Every wonderfully made masterpiece has a starting point. It doesn't start off as a masterpiece, but just as a vision of things to come...

In 2015, I graduated from Eastern Illinois University with honors. I now had a bachelor's Degree in Psychology but didn't have a clue as to what to do with it. I had a new level of respect for myself, but still struggled to find my purpose. With no job, no money, and no real plan for my life, I did what many college students do after they graduate. I moved back home with my parents.

Living at home was not an easy transition for me. If you ever had to move back in with your parents after being on your own, then you know that the struggle is REAL. At the time, my parents had moved away from my childhood neighborhood into a small apartment on the south side of Chicago. I was now away from all of my closest friends, placed in a new environment, had less privacy, and forced to downsize. Imagine being in a situation that is so uncomfortable that the more you analyze it, the more aggravated you become! I felt like no matter what I did, it was impossible for me to adjust to my new living conditions.

Since I had a lot of free time, I spent that summer reading several different books. While searching for a new one to read, I came across one of the graduation presents my mom had given me back in May. If only I had known the *transformational* power that was held within the pages of that book, I would have opened it the second I got it. The book was *Instinct*, by T.D. Jakes. Now, I had read several different types of self-help books, but never one that was *God–centered*.

Have you ever watched something on TV or read something, and felt like the person was speaking DIRECTLY to you? After reading just the first chapter, I was totally convinced that I had expressed to T.D. Jakes how I was feeling, and he wrote this book to help me get through this difficult season. The more pages I turned, the more my entire perspective changed. My eyes opened to new intuitions, possibilities, and revelations that I had never even considered before. The lessons in *Instinct* taught me the fundamentals of being an *effective* adult such as: how to be the best person I can be, how to see the good in every situation, how to develop long-lasting meaningful relationships, how to effectively handle the challenges of adulthood, and most **importantly**...*how to discover my divine purpose in life.*

It is because of this book that I no longer felt hopeless about my situation, but instead *hopefu*l for my future!

Point #1: It's only when you start putting the *right* puzzle pieces together that you'll begin to see the BIG picture.

Imagine trying to complete a puzzle with all the wrong pieces. By the wrong pieces, I mean a bunch of random pieces that didn't match any of the other pieces in the box.

Would you still be able to complete the puzzle?

Remember in the previous chapter, when I shared with you how I felt inadequate because I didn't know what I wanted to do with my life? Well, T.D. Jakes made me realized I couldn't find my purpose because I didn't have the right pieces! Not only that, but I was missing a vital piece. I was missing…*God*. I was running to everyone else in my life, when I should have FIRST run to God! I was trying to put together a clear picture of what Stephanie was created to do with every piece, but the *RIGHT* piece.

The piece that created me.
The piece that knew my future.
The piece that knew exactly what my purpose was.

Take a second to determine what that *BIG picture* for you is. **What is it you want to see manifest in your life?** For me it was finding my purpose. Maybe for you it's a relationship, a career, or your purpose too. Once you have determined what your "big picture" is, ask yourself, *Do I have the* right *pieces needed to make that picture a* reality? Your problem may not be that you aren't *capable* of seeing the BIG picture. It may just be that you don't have the *right* pieces needed to create that particular picture in the first place.

No matter how hard you try, you can't complete a puzzle of a red ball with only blue pieces. Or maybe, just maybe, **you are simply missing *one* key piece that is keeping you from turning that vision into a reality.**

What might that piece be for you?

Is it self-love, a mentor, motivation, or *God?*

Growing up, I was raised in the church, but I never really had a relationship with God. I knew God existed, but I never had a real *encounter* with him. However, after reading *Instinct*, my spiritual eyes began to open, and I formed a desire to know God like never before! Although my ultimate goal was to get God to tell me what my purpose was, He had a *different* goal in mind.

I quickly learned that in order to discover what my God-given purpose was, I had to first know *who* God was. I remember being so obsessed with getting to know him that I spent majority of my time praying, listening to sermons, reading devotionals, and going to church. I became so dedicated to developing an intimate relationship with God, that I went months without really communicating with my friends—and I didn't even notice it! The more I got to know Him, something began to change on the inside of me; something that I couldn't explain. Before I knew it, my thoughts began to change. The way I treated people changed. My interests changed. My entire outlook on life changed. I began to have a new level of peace and satisfaction in my life that I had never experienced before!

I didn't know it at the time, but God wasn't just changing me from the inside out but *molding* me into the woman I was created to be. Besides my mom, my circle had never comprised of *godly* women. None of my friends ever talked about God, and I didn't grow up in a church where I saw God-fearing youth or young adults. My perception of a Woman of God was a super-holy, *older* woman who constantly read her Bible and did nothing but talk to God all day. However, that assumption rapidly changed the day I read the characteristics of what makes a woman a *Woman of God*.

I remember staring at these words in awe.

- *Gentle*
- *Quiet Spirit*
- *Obedient*
- *Kind*
- *Modest*
- *Graceful*
- *Positive*
- *Forgiving*
- *Peaceful*

As I reflected on these words, I felt like I was looking at myself in the *mirror*. It was the perfect reflection of *Stephanie!* This was the first time in my life that I instantly connected with a certain identity. I didn't have *all* the traits, but I had *enough* to feel like I had the potential to truly become a Woman of God. It was not an identity that was forced, nor did it make me uncomfortable. It was natural, like it was who I was born to be!

Here I was thinking that being quiet was weird. I had no idea that it was a *virtuous* characteristic! Just knowing that gave me all the confidence in the world. I was confident that I was no longer going to do things that were contrary to my *new* identity—*my identity as a Woman of God.* When no one was able to help me, God helped me. I was not going to let him down!

I understood that as a Woman of God I was a *representation* of God, and I could no longer just do anything. To become the woman I was created to be, I got rid of my old lifestyle and started creating a new one. Whatever God told me to do, I made sure I did it.

He told me I could no longer listen to certain music or watch certain shows due to their content. So, I cut them out of my life. He told me I couldn't dress in a way that exposed my body, so I walked through my closet one day and pulled out every miniskirt, tight skirt, short shorts, and crop top I had, and gave them away. He told me I could no longer go to night clubs. So I woke up one morning and sent a text to all my friends informing them that I no longer could be a part of the nightclub scene. I was determined to embrace my new identity like my life depended on it.

I was not only embracing who I was, but now *Whose* I was.

Point # 2: A Unique piece wasn't meant to fit in just ANY puzzle.

See, in the past, I was comfortable with being in just *any* puzzle. In my last chapter, I told you that I went with the flow of what everyone else was doing. If my friends wore miniskirts, so did I. If my friends listened to rap music, so did I. If my friends went to the club so did I. However, all of that changed the moment I realized that as a unique puzzle piece, I no longer could fit just *anywhere*, or do just *anything*. I didn't quite understand the change, but I knew I trusted God, and I was determined to stay on the path that He had marked for me.

> *"It's easy to stand in the crowd, but it takes courage to stand alone."* 3
> *–Mahatma Gandhi*

I'm not going to lie to you and say that the journey has been easy, because it hasn't. To be honest, it is one of the scariest and most difficult things I ever had to do in my life! Just put yourself in my shoes. How would you feel? I felt like God was telling me to go back into the world and show people how He changed me…I was terrified! There were times I worried about what other people would think of me.

Will they think I am crazy?
Will they understand me?
Will they accept me?

I know you may want everyone to be supportive in everything you do, but I learned firsthand that isn't going to happen. My new identity has cost me to lose very close friends, including my best friend. Recognize that not everyone *can* or will *want* to go where God is taking you. They may not even *understand* where

God is taking you. Don't let that discourage you! If they want to leave, don't hesitate to let them go.

To grow into the person you are created to be, you have to first die to your old self, and everything that comes with it. You have to be so CONFIDENT in who you are or who you are becoming, that if people aren't already on board, you are not stopping for them. When you start to finally put the pieces of your life together, the last thing you want to do is start picking up old pieces! Continue to move forward, and DON'T look back. Remember, you are on a quest to becoming the person God created you to be. Don't allow distractions to slow you down now!

Take a moment and ask yourself:
What puzzles do I need to get out of?
What pieces are holding me back?
What pieces do I need to let go?

Although I didn't understand what God was doing in my life, I meditated day and night on *one* verse…

"Trust in the LORD with all thine heart and lean not unto thine own understanding. In all thy ways acknowledge him, and he shall direct thy paths."
(Proverbs 3:5-6)

The more I meditated on it, the more I believed it. The more I believed it, the more it manifested!

In a matter of months, God had completely transformed me spiritually, mentally, and physically. I was so amazed by what had happened to me that I developed a burning desire to share my story with others. Since, at the time, I was very active on social media, I started sharing a little bit about my "self-lovery journey" and my relationship with God on Instagram. Now, I didn't expect for anyone to really respond to my posts because I was just expressing myself. However, I got a comment on one of my post one day that read "you are so inspiring!!!"

My immediate thought was, *Me...inspiring?? How can a girl who used to not be able to name five things she loved about herself be "inspiring?"*

At the time I didn't know that they weren't inspired by my brokenness but inspired by my *breakthrough.*

Later that day, I got a text from a friend that read, "Stephanie, I am so proud of you, you have truly blossomed. I can see that you are becoming the woman you were created to be! Keep it up. It's inspiring!

From then on out, I realized that my "story" wasn't just a story, but a *testimony.* To know that I was becoming an inspiration to sooo many women ignited something in me. I wanted to empower women to love themselves, and to start developing a relationship with God. I not only aspired to help women, but girls as well.

In 2016 I created a self-love mentoring program for the girls in my childhood church called *Tiptoeing Forward with Elegance.* The program taught them the fundamentals of being a young lady, learning to love themselves, managing their emotions, and developing effective relationships with others.

Here are a few testimonials from the girls about how they felt about the program:

After being in the program, I feel more confident and comfortable in my own skin, and I am working even harder to put my best foot forward in everything that I do. – MaKayla

Instead of reacting to negativity, I just now let things go. I think back to what you taught me about knowing who I am, and that God has better things in store for me. – Wanderline

Thanks for going out of your way to teach us what it means to be a young lady of God. – Vanica

Thank you, Miss Stephanie! You are a wonderful blessing to all of us!! – All

I was beyond touched by this feedback. I had no idea that I had impacted these girls to that extent! Just knowing that I had the ability to change someone's life, made me begin to see *exactly* what my purpose was.

Point #3 When you recognize that you are a wonderfully made masterpiece, your light will begin to shine!

Once I acknowledged that I was God's wonderfully made masterpiece… other people started seeing it to.

No matter where I went, I would instantly grab people's attention. Literally, random strangers would gaze at me like they were in a gallery and just laid eyes on a *masterpiece*. I remember waiting in line at restaurants and people would just come up to me wanting to know more about me. There was one time I was shopping and a lady, who I had never met before, asked me if I had happened to have some hand sanitizer. I gave her the hand sanitizer and we began to engage in small talk. As I was leaving, she thanked me again and said "man, you are such a sweet and beautiful girl, I wish my son had married a woman like you!"

I remember that day like it was yesterday. I was completely blown away by her comment! I mean, wouldn't you be too? She had only known me for less than *five minutes*! How was she able to make that conclusion about me that quickly? I left the store dumbfounded.

From that day forward, these encounters kept happening more and more...like an everyday routine. No longer was I pushing people away, but I was now *attracting* people to me. No longer were people describing me as bougie and stuck up. Instead, I was described as *elegant* and *confident*. There was something about me that was different, and it captured everyone's attention. My family members, church members, friends, strangers, and even my coworkers started to see the change in me. Some even said that I was beginning to *glow*.

Now, being the introvert that I am, can I be real? I thought it was VERY strange that before I even uttered a word, people were intrigued by me! I felt like I was in *The Twilight Zone*. It was not until I began to write about this experience that I realized I had been so used to being just a *physical* attraction for people, that I never even considered I could be a *spiritual* attraction.

I remember meeting a guy my freshman year at Eastern Illinois University who instantly was attracted to me. Keep in mind that this was the same year I my friends told me I was "bougie." When I asked him why he felt the way he did, he said there was a peaceful elegance about me that he couldn't explain. Now, NO guy had ever described me in such a way before. I instantly thought he was a bit crazy. However, now I see that I have blossomed into the *exact* person he described! Maybe he wasn't crazy after all. He just saw something I didn't see yet...a vision of things to come.

"If you're always trying to be **normal***, you will never* know *how amazing you can be."*₄ Maya Angelou (emphasis added)

As I reflect on the *Wonderfully Made Masterpiece* I have come to be, I often recognize that I am in no way, shape, form, or fashion "normal." Nor do I want to be! Since I started living as a God-fearing woman, my life has never been the same, and I love it! You see, when I would try to be normal and do things everyone else in the world was doing, I felt out of place. Now I see that, as a child of God, I am made to be set apart from this world, not to conform to it.

Oh, and if you were wondering what I love about myself now......

I LOVE that I am confident in my own skin!
I LOVE that I never hold a grudge!
I LOVE that I am an obedient child of God!
I LOVE that I continue to elevate myself to new heights!
I LOVE that I have a heart for seeing other people succeed!

I could go on, but I'll just stop right there.

It was only when I took the time to get to know myself, love myself, then allow God to order my steps, that I discovered that *one thing* I am truly passionate about. I have a burning passion for helping individuals reach their fullest potential in their personal and professional lives. Speaking of which, did I mention that I will be graduating from Lewis University with a Master's Degree in Organizational Leadership on May 20, 2018!? I literally could not have found a better program for me. It's the *perfect* fit.

So now what is my *purpose* you ask?

My purpose is to empower women to be God – fearing ladies who love themselves and have the confidence to achieve anything they set their minds to!

I can't even begin to tell you the blessings and opportunities I have experienced; not because of things I say, things I do, or things I wear, but just because of *who I am*. It's now that I see the light of God is living in me so intensely that it shines right through me! Today I am *walking* in my purpose and people admire my inner beauty, confidence, integrity, and boldness. I didn't know it back then, but I had to go through the journey to realize that I had *always* been a wonderfully made masterpiece all along.

You too are a *Wonderfully Made Masterpiece* and can experience the abundant blessings of God. The only problem is that you don't see it yet. Maybe at this very moment you are feeling like a lost puzzle piece that just can't find its way. You keep trying and trying, but no matter what you do, NOTHING seems to go right for you! Can I tell you something? Whatever your situation is, there is ALWAYS a *light* at the end of the tunnel! For me, God was my light. Maybe He's your light too.

Perhaps you can't even see *any* type of light, because you have *stopped* moving. Or, you have been walking *backwards* and didn't even know it. Yes, I understand you've been hurt. You're confused, you're frustrated, and you just want to give up. BUT if you give up, you will **NEVER** get out of that tunnel! STOP dwelling on your situation and START dwelling in the Lord.

"Delight thyself also in the LORD, and he will shall give thee the desires of thine heart." (Psalm 37:4)

Do you understand that God has a specific assignment for your life? He has a purpose that is specifically unique to your personality, gifts, skills, and abilities. Everything you have experienced in life is not just by coincidence. Your interests, decisions, accomplishments, and even your mistakes…are all clues that can help you piece together your purpose.

God can't guide you out of your tunnel until you start moving. So I challenge you to take that step! If you can't take big steps, then take *baby steps*. It may seem scary at first because you're still seeing darkness. However, I GUARANTEE you that once you start to move in the *right* direction, the picture will begin to get clearer and the light will become brighter! So allow God to guide you, and show you what type of wonderful masterpiece He created YOU to be!

"For I know the thoughts that I think toward you, saith the Lord, thoughts of peace, and not of evil, to give you an expected end." (Jeremiah 29:11.

Behind every successful woman, there is God directing her path.

This is only the beginning!

I hope that my story has inspired you to embrace your own uniqueness, be confident in who you are, and continue to strive to be that *wonderfully made masterpiece* God created you to be! I truly believe you **can** and **will**

147

successfully move from your past into your purpose!! Just by reading this book, you have already made the first step. Keep it up!

Now that you know more about me, I would love to form a relationship with you outside the pages of this book.

So, let's make it happen!

Need someone to talk to? Don't know what to do next? Still feeling like a lost puzzle piece? I want to help you! Let's talk. Contact me.

Email: naturallii.stephanii@gmail.com

Need daily motivation & Christian inspiration? Follow me on Instagram @naturallii_stephanii

Need a guest speaker to empower women or youth? Book me at naturalliistephanii.com

Interested in learning more about me & my services? Visit my website at naturalliistephanii.com1

https://www.goodreads.com/quotes/6565470-don-t-let-someone-else-s-opinion-of-you-become-your-reality
2 https://sites.psu.edu/mnshermanci/
3 http://www.azquotes.com/quote/455993
4 https://www.goodreads.com/quotes/700564-if-you-are-always-trying-to-be-normal-you-will

<u>Meet Stephanie Saintyl</u>

 Stephanie Saintyl is a motivational speaker, youth mentor, and social media influencer. From the moment she realized that simply *loving* herself was the KEY to unlocking the doors to her destiny, she wanted to help other women discover that same *key*. Since 2016, she has been sharing her testimony and empowering girls and women to not let self-doubt, past experiences, or other people cripple them from reaching their fullest potential.

As a natural born speaker, she uses her social media platforms to stir up her followers' faith and draw them closer to God. Every week, Stephanie posts motivational videos that inspire her audience to accomplish their goals and be everything God created them to be. Her professionalism, transparency, and genuineness are what keep them wanting more.

Stephanie has facilitated several women empowerment workshops, and worked closely with teen girls to teach them how to *effectively* implement self -love in their lives. Her innovation and step by step strategies, motivates her audience to take ACTION towards being successful. Her mission is to help teen girls and young women reap the benefits of building an intimate relationship with God…FIRST.

<u>Introducing Daniel and Tara Gazzuolo</u>

When I was away at college, I always loved to receive letters from my friends and family. I felt like I had pen pals who wrote to me, to keep tabs on me and to encourage me. I looked forward to those letters and care packages. There were a lot of times that those care packages provided food or money or even pictures that reminded me someone was thinking of me and that I would make it through this period.

Now imagine not being away at college but being away locked up in prison. Many incarcerated men and women long for pen pals to write to them, put money on their books and encourage them to hold on and be strong. Those letters are the only link to the outside world beyond the walls.

Tara and Dan Gazzuolo know this story all too well. Both have been incarcerated over the course of their lives and did not know each other while being incarcerated. Little did they know that GOD was preparing them for a LOVE BEYOND THE WALLS while they were inside of prison. Dan had no idea that the love of his life was looking at him from a picture inside the locker of his cellmate. Tara had no idea a message of support she was writing to one person would eventually touch the heart of the man she would marry.

In these chapters, Dan and Tara take you on their individual journeys of discovery about themselves that could have only occurred through separation and incarceration. These stories speak to How GOD must separate us from our past to prepare us for the purpose He has in store for us. Dan and Tara both were caterpillars that needed to go into the transformational cocoon, also known as prison, to be fed the necessary spiritual food that would ultimately lead to their butterfly experience!

Now Dan and Tara have a Life and Love Beyond the Walls. Love beyond the walls of Incarceration and prison cells. Love Beyond the walls of self-inflicted pain and suffering. They have a life of self-acceptance, self-forgiveness and higher self-esteem. Now they both have new exciting careers, are both authors and together, they are living testaments to GOD's grace and Mercy and how He can take a Mess and turn it into a Message. They have been able to tear down old walls and do great things beyond those walls. They are 2 ordinary people telling an extraordinary story. We hope that you will see that if they can find Life and Love Beyond the Walls, then YOU CAN TOO! Get ready for another Unstoppable Story of Moving from PAST to PURPOSE!

~ Terrance Leftridge

Chapter 7

Building Walls

What is Love? There are many definitions of what love is. The world says that love is a tender, deep feeling of affection and care toward another person; an intense emotional attachment or feeling for a person, place, or thing.

The Lord expresses His definition of Love (Charity) in I Cor. 13 :4-8a KJV

"Charity suffereth long and is kind; charity envieth not; charity vaunteth not itself, is not puffed up, Doth not behave itself unseemly, seeketh not her own, is not easily provoked, thinketh no evil; Rejoiceth not in iniquity, but rejoiceth in the truth; Beareth all things, believeth all things, hopeth all things, endureth all things. Charity never faileth:"

Comparing these two definitions, love is not feeling, is not emotion, is not attraction, is not having sex, nor is it liking someone. Love is what we do according to the standard of God, not what we feel.

Daniel has learned that love is God's power to change a person. When love is present, healing is made possible. As you read his story you will come to an understanding of why he defines love this way. Tara's definition is similar in the respect that she feels that love is an action. Through realizing she was worthy of love, she found purpose. This enabled her to show love to others. By realizing that she was worthy of love, she opened herself to accept love from others.

Daniel's Story

My story begins behind the walls. They were walls I chose for myself that would keep me safe. Having suffered periods of sexual abuse in my childhood, I quickly learned both to hide and to keep secrets. Little did I know that this would become a defense mechanism that I used well into my adult life. It was comfortable in that lonely place where I hid from the rest of the world. When people got too close to me, I would bail out of the relationship. I'd run from job to job and from place to place. When I got close to someone and let them in, they were then my hostage and I became theirs. I put up with disrespect and abuse just so my place behind the walls wasn't so lonely.

Eventually my loneliness led me to strike out and harm those I loved. This resulted in a 20-year sentence for a crime I will never forget. I would serve 10 years in prison and be required to

YOU ARE **UNSTOPPABLE** *Moving from Past to Purpose*

register my home and work addresses for anyone to view online.

When I was first arrested, I felt like I had been thrown away as a piece of trash. I thought God had abandoned me. I was struggling with guilt and what my punishment should be. Then a volunteer chaplain showed me Hebrews 12:5-13. There the writer of Hebrews explains that God disciplines those He loves. I was conflicted and feeling condemned, but through this passage God showed me that even though I was going to be punished for my crime, and rightfully so, He loved me. This was my first encounter with the unconditional love of God. From that moment on, I knew He would be with me throughout my prison sentence.

God proved Himself faithful and I saw His hand intervene many times. Sometimes God carried me and other times I felt Him right beside me. Toward the end of my sentence, I had a roommate who had a pen pal. He would take out a picture of her and look at it while he wrote the letter. He would then put the picture back into his locker, and every time he opened his locker I would see the picture hanging there. I longed for a pen pal also. I didn't realize it then, but I was looking for a way out of isolation—a way out from behind the walls.

When I was released from prison, I was free on the outside, but I was still incarcerated on the inside. I was full of fear and blamed other people for my situation. Even though I knew God was with me, I felt I was the one who had to make everything happen. Being a registered sex offender caused me to have to move four times in six months. I didn't choose this, but the rules said I had to move. In the following months, I tried to live life on the outside of prison while still living behind the walls on the inside of me. I did not work for over a year. I had few friends that I would let in on my secret. I had forgotten how to speak about the things that were going on inside of me.

One day I got tired of being in hiding. Having just returned from a birthday lunch with my parents, I realized I was alone and in need of help. Instead of trying to find people who would make me feel comfortable in an uncomfortable place, I began looking for relationship—looking for a way out of the darkness. That was when I started to realize how long I had been hiding. All my life I had stubbornly refused to surrender to the process of being in real relationships. I held on to everything I could. It became obvious that I needed a woman in my life and that I needed help to find freedom. So, I got on my knees and prayed asking God in faith for Him to send me a woman I could relate to.

About a month later, I talked to a prison ministry friend. I explained to him about my prayer. He told me about someone he met while ministering in a women's prison. He said that Tara had just been released and was working at Longhorn Steakhouse. He thought I should meet her. When we went to eat she wasn't there, but later he gave her my phone number and she called me.

Our first conversation was over three hours long. We talked a lot about what it was like being in prison and coming out of prison. She shared the same faith that I had, and I could tell she was determined to be successful. We started talking regularly. In fact, she tried to call me several times each day. I started coming out of my shell with her. Here was somebody who had been behind the walls and was now finding freedom. I didn't realize it then, but I was having another encounter with love.

A couple of weeks after our first conversation, Tara showed me some pictures of her. One of them looked familiar, and I suddenly realized that the picture was the same one that was in my former roommate's locker. She was the pen pal! God had answered my prayers. He sent me a woman whose love would lead me out of hiding.

A couple of months later, I had to admit that I was falling in love with Tara. We went to church together and spent time together after church. We talked on the phone a lot and prayed together often. Our first movie date was over the phone. We each found the same movie online and on the count of three we both pressed play. We watched the movie together while talking on the phone about it. My love for Tara was tearing down the walls I had built for so long.

One time she got stuck at my house during a snowstorm. That was the first time I was okay with both being with her for a couple of days and admitting I was ready for her to leave.

It was obvious we were meant to be together. As the months passed, it became harder to say goodbye to her and on March 8, 2011, I proposed to her. We decided that we would remain abstinent until we got married and were successful in fulfilling that commitment. We continue to celebrate our God-directed marriage.

Today I can say that I like living outside my walls. Tara's love and the love of God have brought me out to a place of true freedom. I can be comfortable in a crowd or by myself. I'm okay talking or being quiet and I don't just love others, I love myself.

Tara's Story

My story is like Dan's in the respect that I built walls to hide behind. I was the youngest of three. As a small child I had to fight to make myself heard. At a very young age, I began to feel unwanted. As in many families, being the baby, they took less pictures of me than of my brother and sister. My sister teased me and told me that I was adopted. I know now that she meant no harm, but my little mind took her seriously. Adding to this, I had a teacher in third grade who I remember ridiculing me in front of the class. She called me stupid and said I would never amount to anything. Her words that day set into motion a path I would walk for the next 30 years.

At the age of five, my mother developed a life-threating illness, and the structure of our family changed forever. She was no longer able to care for us on a full-time basis. Because of this, my siblings and I were shuffled between caregivers daily. Being so young, I didn't understand fully what was going on and felt that I must somehow be responsible. All of this added to the feelings of unworthiness, being unwanted and less than enough.

As a small child I had to fight to make myself heard. This lead to a lifestyle of seeking attention and always wanting to be in the limelight. I felt that I needed to earn the approval of those around me and the only way to do that was to be good enough. I was never able to obtain that goal, even though I was the only one who expected it.

In the summertime each year, we would go to our grandmother's house. It was there that a period of abuse began. I had no idea that my brother had been sexually abusing my sister. As a self-protection measure, she asked my brother to please leave her alone and to "bother Tara." For the next six years, I was a victim in my own home. I was not able to tell anyone because I again felt it was my fault, and that somehow, I had caused this to happen.

On the surface, our family appeared to be the perfect family. I remember an instance when my sister and I were arguing in the front yard. The neighbors were shocked and called their girls saying, "Wow, the Hassell's do fight." Until that point we had been able to hide the ugliness we were living in.

In my quest to be the "best," I excelled at many of the things I was a part of outside of the home. The main activity that consumed my time was singing.

I "fell in love." Finally, something I was good at and others acknowledged it. Voice lessons began, and I joined the chorus at school, singing solos at church. All this fed my attention-seeking desire and thrust me into the limelight. Since I felt this was the only thing I was good at, naturally it led to my majoring in voice performance at college.

What I haven't shared to this point is that I tried to sabotage any success I had. My feelings of unworthiness, lack of self-worth, and feelings of being unloved were stronger than my desire for accomplishment. An example of this is when I met my first husband. He was the only person who ever said he loved me. I realize now that he just wanted to have sex. All my attention turned to that relationship. I no longer wanted anything but to be a wife. My identity was no longer Tara. I lost myself in him. I thought that being loved by someone else was the answer. What I still didn't realize was that I hated myself.

Three short months after becoming a wife, my identity changed again. I was becoming a mother. Finally, I was going to have someone to love who would love me just for me. My daughter was born, and I thought that all my hurts and struggles were over. Little did I know how wrong I was.

All the wounds, scars, and hurts from my past had affected me to the point that I was not capable of being the wife or mother I could have been. I still wanted to have all the attention and be in the limelight.

My husband had a seizure disorder and his health became a way to gain attention. My daughter had an issue with her ability to clear her sinuses, which led to frequent trips to the doctor. That also became an avenue for gaining attention. For the third time my identity was changing. I was becoming the caregiver.

In my efforts of trying to be perfect, I again failed. My daughter got very ill due to my negligence, which led to my being accused of intentionally harming her. The next three years were spent trying to prove that was I was innocent. I was unaware that the State was investigating me for criminal charges. I was arrested for cruelty to children in 2001, and in 2003 I accepted a "no contest" plea of 12 years to serve 8 in prison. I was exhausted and just wanted it all to end.

My new identity was "inmate." When you enter the walls of a prison, you lose everything. In my case, that was truer than I ever imagined it could have been. Six weeks after entering prison, my husband moved out of state and six months later filed for divorce. Eighteen months into my sentence my mother passed away, and I didn't hear from my siblings again until my release.

I quickly realized I was not going to survive as an inmate if I didn't make some serious changes. Throughout my incarceration, I took a hard look at myself and took responsibility for my actions. Even though what happened was not intentional, it was due to my negligence. I was responsible after all. I had to realize this valuable truth, accept it, and move on to find my purpose. I once had an overwhelming need for attention, always wanting to be noticed. I have learned that I do not have to do anything to gain the attention or approval of others, just being me was, and is, enough. The only approval I need is that of my Lord and, through the saving grace of the cross, that approval was granted.

I took a group called Moral Recognition Therapy (MRT); which became the catalyst for my change to begin. I also participated and completed the Faith & Character Based Program. While in that program I took a class called Confronting Self. I had to face some things head on. That was a hard thing to do, because facing the truth and knowing that you must change is hard work. I had to learn things about myself I did not recognize. There were things I had kept buried, things I was in denial about and just did not want to face. I had to learn to stop putting everyone else's needs before my own and start living a life that embraces personal purpose.

That purpose is an exercise of caring for my best and most important asset—ME! I must be ready always to make the necessary changes so that the finished product is brand new. The old ideas, habits, and behaviors had been erased. The new "I" was ready to emerge. None of this would have been possible without my being plugged into the power source of the Holy Spirit. Learning to listen to His leading and guidance is the greatest tool I have had.

I started by setting little goals, things I could do daily and accomplish something that would help with my transformation. Every day was a new day to do something different just for me. I had to develop a sense of authority over my past, an appreciation for the present, and confidence in the journey toward my future. I am the only person who defines me. Self-determination is a power I own.

To be something I have never been, I must be willing to do something I have never done. I dared to be and do something new. I started allowing the Lord to change me from the inside out. This was not possible under my own ability. I had to surrender the control to Him. I could no longer live my life based on the expectations, choices and opinions of others.

I learned I could no longer let the nouns (people, places, and things) cheat me out of what I was put here on this earth to do. I had to develop a vision and move toward satisfying it. Even if my vision changes, I know I will gain valuable insight that will lead me to my appropriate destination. Despite what did or did not happen yesterday, today is a beginning.

I have moved from the old comfort zones and created new ones that allow me to change and grow. I have learned to explore, dream, and discover. I have learned that it's the trials, tribulations and struggles that strengthen us. I look back now and see my Heavenly Father's hand guiding me in times when I thought no one was there. "Be strong and courageous. Do not be afraid or terrified because of them for the Lord your God goes with you, He will never leave you nor forsake you" (Deuteronomy 31:6, NIV) has become alive to me. I know that He not only is with me, but that He goes before me to prepare the way for me.

I am, for the first time in my life, confident of Whose I am, what I am, and who I am. I am

YOU ARE **UNSTOPPABLE** *Moving from Past to Purpose*

excited about what the future holds and what the Lord has in store for that future. I answer to a higher calling now, one that only He can give.

Returning home as a new person was not easy. During my time in prison so many things had changed in the world and in me. I was moving in with my brother, I had no job, and was going to an entirely new city. What I did have was connections that I had made while I was in prison. Dan always says, "Our greatest assets are people," and it was during this time that this became true for me.

One of the first things I was determined to do after release was to reconnect with a prison ministry team which I had grown very close to while incarcerated. I reached out to Burning Bush Ministries to make that connection.

Don and Genene always said, "When you come home we would be honored to have you visit with us at our church." It was on my birthday in 2010 that Don shared the phone number of a gentleman who also had been released and had connected with them. Don thought it would be good for me to have someone who understood what I was going through and I could talk with. Three days later I found the courage to call Dan, and a relationship began that would eventually lead to dating, engagement, and marriage.

I had no idea when I made that call I would be talking with the man God had been preparing for me to spend the rest of my life with. Dan and I shared many things in common. We both had been raised in middle class families, both were music majors in college, we both were victims of sexual abuse as children, and we both had been in prison. Also, we both knew how to hide behind walls. It wasn't easy to learn how to allow someone in, nor was it easy to learn to love again. I had to let go of old baggage from other relationships and from my former marriage. Through the grace of God, our relationship grew into what it has become today.

Chapter 8

Walls Falling Down

Our story began with us both behind walls. Walls that were built from years of neglect and the physical walls of prison. Beginning a relationship with each other began to expose the walls we each had built. Follow along on our journey as we started tearing down those walls.

Tara: I was able to tear down the wall of not being lovable. My wall of not being good enough began to crumble the more our relationship grew. I was beginning to understand that nothing defined me, especially a relationship. I was good enough just because the Lord said I was.

Dan: While I was in prison I was isolated. Even though I had people to talk to, I remained distant. Sometimes I would get to know someone and then they would be transferred to another prison or released. This resulted in my choosing to stay to myself. By the time I was released I had unknowingly become hardhearted. I spent my first year trying to live outside of prison the same way I lived on the inside. When I met Tara, I discovered that I had to start living differently.

Tara: Dan was beginning to show me that he loved me for who I was. I didn't have to "be" what he wanted. He loved me and cared about what I loved. I remember sharing with Dan just how trapped I felt. I expressed my sadness at seeing dandelions outside of my window and that I wasn't even able to blow them. I told him that as a child it was one of my favorite things to do. Several days later we were again talking. Dan told me to hang on, and the next thing I heard was him blowing a dandelion. It was in that moment I knew he cared deeply about what I said. He listened to me and took notice. My wall of feeling ignored was torn down.

Dan: I gradually began to let Tara in. From our first conversation, I knew there was something special about her. If I was going to relate to her I would need to allow my walls to come down. This is what God was leading me into. He knew that finding Tara would force me to open up. At first, I was annoyed by Tara's constant calls. After talking it over at my support group, I realized it was an opportunity to tear some walls down.

Tara: One of the most difficult walls I had built was that of "being noticed." All my life I wanted someone to say I was doing good or that I was important. Even though I was much better than before I went to prison, I still felt that I had to "make things happen" to get noticed. My calls to Dan became a plea to be loved. Little did I know that I was falling into an old habit of ruining the good things that were happening in my life. Dan did not have to hear from me every few hours to know that I cared, nor should I have had to hear from him. Slowly, I was able to let down the wall of insecurity and to trust Dan. There was a period of about a week that Dan didn't want to hear from me. I was devastated. Dan, on the other hand, just needed to breathe. This experience caused me to understand fully that Dan loved me and wanted to have a lasting relationship with me. He loved me enough to take the time he needed alone so that we would be better together.

Dan: When Tara and I first met in person I would not sit next to her. I was afraid of her. I took a week-long trip to the Georgia mountains to sort out my feelings for her. During that week, I had no contact with anyone. After much prayer and soul-searching, I accepted that I loved her. I went to a fast food restaurant to connect to the Wi-Fi and watch our live church service. I saw Tara singing in the choir and began to cry. Very soon thereafter, I admitted my love to her.

Tara: We began sharing life together. Dan and I were committed to having a godly relationship and were very careful about intimacy.

We were intentional about keeping physical boundaries. It was getting harder and harder to be apart. The first Christmas we dated, Dan asked me to spend the holiday with his family. He put up a little tree in his apartment and his mother even made a stocking with my name on it. It was becoming clear to me that I was a part of his life. During that holiday, we had our first real argument. The neat thing about it was it didn't ruin what we were building, and I was able to move past it. I knew Dan loved me and that I couldn't destroy his love. I felt a sense of belonging that I had never felt before.

Dan: Over time I allowed Tara to be a bigger part of my life. We spent more time together doing life. We enjoyed movies, time in front of the fireplace, and playing games together. We spent a few days together during a snow storm, sleeping in separate rooms. It became difficult to have to say goodbye to her. Then on March 8, 2011, Tara was leaving my apartment and I did not want to say goodbye. I knew that I wanted to be with her for the rest of my life. So, standing at my front door, I asked her to marry me. Of course, she said yes, and I immediately called everyone I knew. Not only had the walls come down, but I was stepping into my new freedom.

Tara: When Dan asked me to marry him I knew life was about to change. We both were committed to being in some sort of ministry. At the time, I don't think either one of us knew what our purpose was. I did know that Dan was to play an important role in discovering mine. He became my biggest cheerleader. Dan encouraged me to step beyond my fears and go after my passions. I wanted to give back to those still behind the walls. Dan embraced my ideas and helped me collect 2600 bars of soap to send into the prisons at Christmas. He celebrated my wins as if they were his and shared my pain when I fell.

I was beginning to get a glimpse of how powerful we would be together when we put the Lord first in our lives. The image of a triangle came to mind. Dan at one corner, myself at the other and the Lord at the top. As we both grew closer to the Lord we grew closer to each other. Ecclesiastes 4:12 KJV states "And if one prevails against him, two shall withstand him; and a threefold cord is not quickly broken..." As part of our wedding ceremony, we braided a cord of three strands. A blue one to represent Dan, yellow for me and in the middle, white, to represent the Lord. Our marriage is at its strongest when we keep the Lord at the center. To remind us of this, each year on our anniversary we braid a little bit more of our cord.

Dan: When I stepped from the altar at our wedding I was confident that I had made the right decision. I never thought there would be such freedom in accepting responsibility. As soon as we returned from our honeymoon, this confidence was tested. Our new neighbors discovered that I am on the Georgia Sex Offender Registry and told our landlord. He told us that we had to move, but I stood my ground and refused to consider the place as anything but our home. Seven years later we are still in the same home and our landlord is a friend.

God used Tara to change me from being isolated and lonely into being free to make healthy choices for myself. I chose to become a certified volunteer with the Georgia Department of Corrections. Three years from the day I was released, I walked back into Johnson State Prison to share my experience and offer hope. The Lord used me that night and I am grateful. Since then I have overcome the fear of being looked down upon for my past.

Tara: The one thing I want you to take away from my story is that there is a purpose for what you are experiencing. The bad and the good—all of it—is shaping and molding you to step into your calling. I can look back at my past and see ways that the Lord was weaving His will into my life. He was and is always there. When trying to understand the purpose behind the pain I went through, I see how it fits in my purpose in life. If I had not been willing to move from my past, I never would have discovered my purpose. My purpose is to share the trials and triumphs that the Lord has allowed in my life to offer hope to those who feel that they have no hope. I share my experiences to keep others from having to go through similar hurts. Revelation 12:11a KJV says "And they overcame him by the blood of the Lamb, and by the word of their testimony;"

Dan: I have come a long way by the grace of God living a daily walk of discovery. I'm still learning what my purpose is and walking through every door that opens. Instead of being secluded from the world I am fearlessly facing life and have found that my faith keeps me strong through life's ups and downs. I have joined the worship team at my church. Later this year I will be leading a small group in my home and traveling on a mission trip. God continues to bring me further away from my past and to give me more opportunities to prove I am a new man. "Therefore, if any man be in Christ, he is a new creature: old things are passed away; behold, all things are become new." (II Corinthians 5:17 KJV)!

Moving from past to purpose looks different for everyone. In our case the journey was similar in that we both had to break down the walls that had held us back. We had to face fears, struggles and obstacles, some of our own making. The key is that we faced them and moved past them. Had we not been willing to do so we would have become like a pond that has no movement, stagnate.

Our prayer for you is that you can find the strength to leave your past behind and have the courage to step into your God given purpose.

"and we know that all things work together for good to them that love God, to them who are the called according to his purpose." (Romans 8:28 KJV).

<u>Meet the Gazzuolo's</u>

 Daniel and Tara Gazzuolo desire to bring positive change to everyone they encounter. They use their life experiences to inspire, encourage and uplift. Both convicted felons, they have moved beyond their past and are passionate about helping others find freedom.

Having both been incarcerated, they met after being released and soon were married. They became involved in prison ministry together and began speaking about the changes they have made in their lives.

Daniel is an entrepreneur. He is active in the Praise Team at his church and is a small group leader. He has spoken on several occasions sharing his story of redemption and renewal to those still behind bars.

Tara is the owner of Butterfly Grafix, a graphic design business in Woodstock, Georgia. She has had the privilege of working with clients from all over the country. To visit Butterfly Grafix go to www.butterflygrafix.com.

She also frequently speaks inside the Georgia prison system sharing her story of transformation. She is also the author of *"Becoming a Butterfly... A treasury of thoughts by Tara."*

Daniel and Tara have begun Love Beyond the Walls, an organization designed to help those who are struggling to find freedom.

For more information on booking Daniel and Tara for your next event or speaking engagement, contact them at info@lovebeyondthewalls.com

Introducing Marie Abega

In the PAST, I can remember being insecure. I can remember feeling like for people to like me, I had to try to fit in. I was short, not tall so I didn't fit in with most of the kids in my class. I was not athletic, so I didn't fit in with the popular kids. So, I had to tap into other talents like music, intellect and sometimes sarcasm to make my mark or impression on the people in my circle of influence. I had to learn to be whoever I needed to be to navigate the situations I found myself in.

This is Marie Abega's story as well, but to a different extreme. Like me, Marie found herself trying to fit into her surroundings. Unlike me, she had to do it on 2 Continents, 5 states and 12 cities over 20 years. Being born in a different country and coming to a new world created her 1st opportunity to fit in and over the course of her life, more than 1200 opportunities have arisen. The problem is when you spend more time trying to fit into other people's world; you rarely have time to find out who you are.

Marie talks about the "Chameleon effect" in her chapters and what long term damage it can do to a person. Her past was one of loneliness and acquiescence. Now she knows she was created to

Stand Out! She is in love with herself and wants to teach others how to express Self Love.

Keep reading this truly Unstoppable story of MOVING from PAST to PURPOSE!

Chapter 9
Lost Identity (The Chameleon Effect)

The Chameleon Effect: A Fluctuating Identity. The manifestation of a basic inability or difficulty in establishing a "stable sense of self." Sarah Myles and the name of the article

The chameleon effect is a borderline personality disorder. It is the constant unconscious change in a person's self as they struggle to fit in with the environment or the people around them. According to Sarah Myles, who wrote an article on the chameleon effect (https://sjmyles79.wordpress.com/2013/07/22) , it is essentially a *fluctuating identity*. It is the manifestation of a basic inability or difficulty in establishing a stable sense of self.

Before I continue to dive into the chameleon effect, I want you to understand why you are reading about this. You may know people in your life that you don't quite understand. They may have a fluctuating personality or a low sense of self. I want you to picture that friend who gets along with everyone and can fit into many different groups of people. We all have that one friend. I was that friend, and it may even be you. I was that girl, "The Social Butterfly." Throw me anywhere, and just like a chameleon, I could camouflage and look like everyone in the group. Crazy, right? I know you have watched that friend and asked yourself, "How *does he/she do that"?* You may have even distanced yourself from people like this due to lack of understanding and inconsistency. I want to shed some light on the chameleons in your life, even if it's you.

I was born in Cameroon, in West Africa, and from what I can remember, that little girl back there was vibrant, happy, sassy, bubbly, friendly, and loving, and well-loved by those around her. I was the girl you could find playing soccer with the boys outside in the mud while it rains, but I was also the girl you could find playing dress up in the house with the girls. Now, Cameroon is divided into two regions, The "Anglophones" or the English side and the "Francophones" or the French side.

Fortunately for me, my parents are from both sides. My mother represented the English side and my father the French. These are two extreme groups. They behave differently and speak differently. They have different cultures, dress differently, and believe in different things. Now, you can imagine how this could be confusing to a child. Although there are great advantages of being from both groups, there are also great disadvantages. The first and obvious advantage was being able to speak more than one language. Another one is exposure to both cultures. The obvious disadvantage was the confusion it caused in my young mind, having to separate the two cultures and know how to behave in the two households. I had to learn how to adapt all the time.

At some point during my childhood, I want to say about the age of five, my mother had a near-death experience that caused her to move to the US for medical care. After she left, my younger brother and I were in the care of my father and my maternal grandmother. I just want you to understand how extremely different these two households were. At my father's house, I was the center of attention. I was called "princess" because, according to them, I am an heir of the land in Cameroon. My dad's family, also of Spanish descent, helped build Yaoundé, in the French side, and also the capital of, Cameroon. My father was extremely important, well-known and well-respected. I was often also treated as such by everyone on that side.

My aunts and uncles there treated me like royalty, as my dad and his family own most of the land in Yaoundé. Here, I was spoiled beyond measures. What I wanted was what I got. I was my dad's side pocket; he did nothing without me. I was in heaven at his house. I remember waking up to him sitting by my bedside, looking at me like his princess. Here, though, I didn't have many friends. I was sheltered, I had a large family and they all lived next door to each other. We had a whole street of houses that belonged only to family members. My cousins were my friends. If I wasn't with my dad, I was at a family member's house within walking distance.

Now, at my maternal grandmother's house, the house was packed. It was a big, gated house guarded by a German shepherd named Denver. All my aunts and uncles on my maternal side lived in this home with their kids. It seemed as though people slept everywhere in the house—on the floor, the couch, the hallways—just everywhere. I remember some nights sleeping on the bed with my grandmother. We had at least ten people in this house. But it was fun here, a different kind of fun from my father's house.

Here, everyone was too busy doing their own thing. No one was the center of attention here. Everyone here worked hard. We woke up early in the morning to help my grandmother prepare for the market. She was the breakfast/early lunch cook for the students and the community there. We were also well-known here. Everyone loved my grandmother's food. I loved my grandmother's hustl and often hung around her, listening to stories and wise tales she lovingly shared with me. I often helped her in the market. At home, a big pot of food was cooked, and we often ate together and shared everything.

Not everyone was nice in this house. As children, we knew whom we could talk to, who didn't have time, and whom we could trust and whom we couldn't. Here, I had friends and I had the freedom to go to their houses and play with them. They were also in walking distance. But I was more like that cool friend who comes and visits, then leaves for a while. In the house, no one really paid attention, no one really cared too much. I remember arguing with my brother to the point that we got into a physical brawl. My uncles and aunts just sat there and watched as entertainment. This would have never happened in my father's house. It was a bit rougher here but fun and strengthening.

I often flip-flopped between these two towns and homes, having to change my whole personality from one house to the other to be accepted and understood. I believe this was the beginning of my chameleon. I never felt completely accepted with either group, unlike those who spent all their time there. I wasn't always there, and so I couldn't always relate. This chameleon began to take many more forms, shapes, and colors when I moved to the United States. At 11, my mom finally sent for us to be reunited with her.

Just like in Cameroon, I found myself living the same type of life in my new country, but this time it was worse. I wasn't born here. No one knew my family like they did back home. The US is much bigger, and my mom constantly moved from apartment to apartment. We had no stable home. I found myself constantly trying to fit in with different groups, different ethnicities, and different cultures. My first language was French, and now I had to learn American English, which was different from what little English I knew from British speakers.

In the past 20 years, I have lived in 12 cities and 5 states, giving me 1200 "unique" opportunities to change my personality.

"You can never Fit In when you were created to Stand Out." Although I had 1200 opportunities to change my personality to fit in, fitting in never worked. You see, in every city and state I lived in, the culture was extremely different, and I had learned the art of adapting. I knew how to change my color, my appearance, my language, my laugh, and just like a chameleon, I knew how to camouflage well.

I must admit, my ability to camouflage and change my personality made me feel powerful and popular until that, too, no longer worked. You see, for borderlines, everything stems from lack of stable self, and a lack of my stable self was starting to cost me. I began to surround myself with people who were sure of themselves—people who had a consistent track record. You see in business, you need to show consistency, and as a chameleon, being consistent was more difficult for me.

I once again had to learn to adapt, but this time for a more stable self. Borderlines instinctively mirror to fit in, because without that behavior, we have no sense of our own identity. We don't know if we will be accepted by others. Without acceptance we risk abandonment, an intense fear for borderlines. Why? Because if we are abandoned, we have no one to mirror. Sarah Myles said it this way,

"It is terrifying to be left alone with yourself.

When you don't know who your self is."

Imagine being alone, looking into a mirror, and seeing a total stranger, or even worse, seeing nobody at all. I remember at different stages of my life looking in the mirror and thinking to myself, *Who are you?* I am grateful that today, I have acknowledged the presence of my chameleon. Identifying my chameleon helped me make sense of a lot things. It helped me understand my habits and why I was the way I was. My chameleon explains why I had a fear of being alone. Why, as an adult, I experience severe dissociation, why I can be so aloof, and why I attempt to exert control over my external life, even though internally there is a lot of chaos.

It explains why I am regarded by others as something of a "social butterfly," constantly fitting from group to group, person to person, and being different things to different people as required. It explains my inability to say "no," and why my persona changes depending on whom I interact with—even down to my accent and mannerisms. These are not conscious behaviors, though. I've begun to catch my chameleon in action.

It is only through awareness that the chameleon can be managed. I say "managed" because, is my chameleon completely gone? No! But it is soothing to have explanations and answers. You may know a chameleon in your life. You may even be that chameleon. And, like me, you may have lost your true identity trying to fit in. There may be a chameleon in your life. You may identify with some of the behaviors I have listed above and wonder how you too can learn to manage your chameleon.

If the problem is an unstable sense of self, the answer is to build a more stable one. It is time to stop running from you who are. It is time to own up to, accept, and embrace everything about you. There can never be a copy of you. You are the real YOU! Although a chameleon may be called a borderline personality disorder, it is to me also a gift. A gift of being able to adapt to any situation life throws at you. Many people don't have that gift, but you do or know someone who does. When you can accept and acknowledge this gift, you can manage it. You can help others find their chameleon.

A common quote that has been uttered by famous people such as Wayne Dyer and Steve Jobs says,

> *"If you change the way you look at things, the things you look at will change."*

I changed the way I viewed my chameleon, and everything else changed. I learned to embrace the chameleon that lives within me, and you can too. It was through self-awareness and self-love that I learned to manage my chameleon.

In the next chapter, I will define self-awareness and self-love and give the tips and tools I used to help me create a stable sense of self. I will share with you how self-awareness, self-love and acceptance helped me move from my past to my purpose. I promise you, you can do it too.

Chapter 10
Finding Total Self-Love in My purpose

According to the Oxford dictionary, Self-awareness is the conscious knowledge of one's own character, feelings, motives, and desires. It is defined as the accurate appraisal and understanding of your abilities and preferences and their implications for your behavior and their impact on others. It is the knowledge of self—strengths and weaknesses, vulnerabilities and passions. Self-awareness is a lifelong journey because you will never stop learning and finding new things about you if you choose to be aware. It can take years to find out who you really are, where you belong, and what you can best contribute to others. Thankfully, some of us have been given opportunities to test our skills and see our impact.

Self-awareness helps us become more aware of our potential and how we naturally behave in specific situations like

- Are you good in crises, or do you provoke them?
- Are you really emotionally intelligent?
- Why do certain types of people clearly not like you?

- Are you aware of what stresses you and what your fundamental values are?
- Are you self-conscious in the sense that you really have self-understanding?
- Do you know your true value and place in the world?
- What clearly makes you extremely happy?
- What is your love language?
- What parts do you play in your self-concept?

If you can answer most of these questions without hesitation, then you are very aware. But, self-awareness doesn't end there. Remember I said earlier in the text that it is a lifelong journey and there are many levels of it. Becoming aware of everything about me is how I found myself again. It is how I regained my power. I learned about the chameleon habits in me. I learned that I had to set new boundaries, I learned that certain behaviors I had were self-destructive. I also learned that I was very strong and courageous.

Becoming aware took me back to my childhood, back to the playground. Now it is your turn. In order to move from your past to your purpose, you will have to be more aware of who you are, what makes you valuable, and why you should care. I once heard Oprah say on TV "*As you become more clear about who you really are, you'll be better able to decide what is best for you -the first time around.*" Think about this quote for a second. This means if you are not clear about who you are, you will not be able to decide what is best for you the *first* time.

The key to your best life is in your ability to decide and commit to what is best for you. Are you willing to commit to discovering you and what is best for you? Are you willing to make the necessary adjustments to move from your past to purpose? Are you ready for the healing process that comes with self-awareness? I believe you are because you are still reading.

Here are tips and tools to bring more awareness into your life.

Here is a fun tool. Let's do a **self-awareness test**.

Take a piece of paper, and make a list of five things for each

- Your five weaknesses
- Your five strengths
- The five-pivotal people who have made a difference in your life
- The five big moments in your life

Now, answer these questions as honestly as you can.

1. Who am I?

2. Why am I here?

3. What do I like and why?

4. What do I dislike and why?

5. What are my hobbies and how do they improve my life?

6. What are my insecurities?

7. What do I want out of life? How am I going to do it?

8. What does my best day look like? How can I create it?

9. What are my beliefs?

10. Do I have boundaries for every important area of my life? Yes or No (circle one) If yes, what are they? If no, let me create them because boundaries help me protect my space and my energy.

11. What are my goals? (List short- mid- long-term.)

12. How is who I am today affecting my future self?

13. What is my self-concept?

14. Are my relationships meaningful?

Let's do a relationship test.

Do you agree or disagree with the following?

1. My relationships help to lessen my loneliness.
2. My relationships help me gain self-knowledge and in self-esteem.

3. My relationships help enhance my physical and emotional health.
4. My relationships maximize my pleasures and minimize my pains.
5. My relationships help me secure stimulation (intellectual, physical and emotional).

When it comes to relationships, we have the hardest time choosing what is best for us because of the attachments we may have with certain individuals. I know you didn't answer "agree" to all the statements above, but it should be a goal as you move from your past to your purpose. Remember, it is a process.

I know that to move from your past to your purpose, you will have to know and embrace who you are and be unapologetic about it.

You cannot serve others from an empty cup. You must work on being the best version of yourself every day, and on loving *every* version of you. Understand that each last version of you is the prerequisite for your next version.

Now, self-love really helped me embrace all my findings, heal, and recreate myself. Self-love is defined as regard for one's own well-being and happiness. However, many of us spend time looking for happiness first in others and give up the power we have within ourselves to be happy and whole. I had completely given up my power at one point. Giving up my power left me powerless, causing me to shrink. I blamed myself and was ashamed of my past and mistakes. I understood that I needed to get rid of this feeling and heal. But how? How could I heal? I was broken, frustrated, saddened by my failed relationship. I was always the pretty girl with all her stuff together; at least, so it seemed.

God gave me a word and I kept hearing self-love in my spirit. I started doing research and began to understand that self-love was my answer to healing. You see, with self-love, you must dig so deep within yourself. You must forgive yourself and learn how to cherish and accept the person in the mirror. You must fall into an unconditional relationship with yourself. You must be aware of everything that makes you unique and understand your F.O.R. (frame of reference) and those of others. I had to find who I was, what made me valuable in this world, my gifts and talents, my likes and dislikes. EVERYTHING! And THAT is how I was able to find myself again. Was this an easy journey? Absolutely Not! Let me explain why.

You see, it may be hard to accept that you have participated in your own self-hate or detrimental behaviors. You may find it hard to accept that you have let yourself down sometimes. You will have to cry away the guilt and shame you have placed on yourself. Crying may make you feel weak, but crying is one of the highest forms of healing. You will have to forgive yourself for your past mistakes and embrace that part of you also. Understand that self-love doesn't make you perfect; it helps you learn to love how perfectly imperfect you are.

I have gained so much insight on self-love and its importance in life. I have branded myself as the Self-Love Strategist, and I am so excited to use the rest of this chapter for actions steps on how you can use Self-Love in your daily life, and how it can help you move from your past to your purpose. Before I go into the tips and strategies, I wanted to share some of the benefits with you.

- **Health.** When you love yourself, you make the right and healthy choices for your better self. You have great self-care habits.
- **Relationships.** When you love yourself, you build authentic relationships, you build boundaries, and only accept the love you deserve from others.
- **Confidence Booster.** When you love yourself, you are confident, but not egotistic.

You aim for things that bring you more self-respect.

- **Style/Swag.** When you love yourself, you have this unique style and swag that is attracting to others. You tend not follow the crowd.

- **Courageous.** When you love yourself, you tend to be more courageous and assertive when it comes to getting your needs met. You are not a people pleaser. You protect your energy and your space.

- **High drive and motivation.** When you love yourself you tend to stay motivated. You do things that bring you to your higher self. Motivation and a hard drive to accomplish your goals are needed to be your higher self.

To find my freedom, I prayed for guidance. God opened a new door for me in Houston. I gave up everything I knew and had up to that point and moved to Houston. My flight to Houston was the most freeing experience I have had in my life. I felt a huge weight lift off and an immense happiness and a peace I still can't fully explain today came over me. I experienced each of the points above. It was then that I moved from my past to my purpose.

In Houston I took a healing path and, for the first time in my life, I understood what it really meant to love myself. Here, I was free to be self, my true self—that happy, vibrant, goofy five-year-old that I remembered. I was safe again. I had regained all my power. I took my power back from the world. I recreated myself, not to something new this time to fit in, but to who I was meant and created to be. It wasn't all easy and sunny. I had to look in the mirror daily and affirm myself.

Here are some Self-Love Affirmations I use daily!

- I am beautiful inside and out
- I am a worthy person
- I am responsible
- I am capable of loving
- I can accept my past but also let it go
- I can assert myself when appropriate
- I can control my anger
- I will get over my guilty feelings
- I will study more effectively
- I will not take on more responsibility than I can handle

In addition to these affirmations, I worked hard on me for two years before moving to Houston, and the hard work was starting to pay off. Within six months of being in Houston, I completed my very first book. The freedom you gain when moving from past to purpose is priceless. I promise you, there isn't a price you can ever place on that.

Now, I want you, right where you are, to imagine your being free. Imagine letting go of your past. I want you to imagine your freedom place. What does that look like for you? Where would you travel? How will you feel? Who will be there with you? What will your day be like? And your night? Write it all down.

Now what sacrifice are you willing to make for this freedom? You see, there is a price for freedom. Freedom comes with a sacrifice. I sacrificed my old life to regain myself. I had to let go of everything I had built in a lie and rebuild in truth. Think about your life now, the identity you carry now. Is that really you? Are you living in your truth? Have you accepted your story? That is the only way you can get to your purpose. There are no shortcuts. My coach and mentor Dr. Ruben West says "you cannot consistently be who you are not." Your purpose requires consistency in who you are, hard work, and dedication.

Seven Ultimate Steps for Your Self-Love Journey

1. **Choose you.** Become aware of who you are and make a commitment to choosing you. Commit to practicing mindfulness every day. Becoming mindful of what you think, feel, and want. Mindfulness is the key to

making sound decisions and the fundamental competency of emotional intelligence.

2. **Develop the Ultimate Relationship.**
   Develop a genuine relationship with your Creator first, then with yourself, and, finally, with other individuals who have common goals. Your relationship with your Creator will guide and direct you to all truth. The individuals that are assigned to journey with you on the course towards purpose and destiny are revealed through a bona fide connection with God. Don't travel alone.

3. **Be You.** There is no one out there who can consistently be you. Only you can do that. God only created one of you. Your personality, gifts, talents, and abilities are different from others'. Understand that you are the only one who can fulfill your assignment. When you begin to love yourself unconditionally, you will begin to form an unconditional love for life and each experience you have.

4. **Fear not.** Fear is inevitable. It is also fake evidence appearing real. You have a head start because you know what it is. The enemy uses the deception of fear to intimidate you from manifesting passion and purpose. The Bible, my favorite book, tells me, "For God hath not given us the spirit of fear; but of power, and of love, and of a sound mind. (2 Timothy 1:7 KJV). Do not abort your future by allowing fear to regulate and preside over your life.

5. **Embrace Failures.** Wisdom is gained and lessons are learned through painful experiences, mistakes, and failed situations. Embrace them. Think of failures as your alert system. They help you redirect your route to something better.

6. **Develop an Attitude of Gratitude.** Do not become so consumed with what is wrong that you are no longer grateful for what is going well. Make a conscious decision to recognize the blessings in your life. I personally adopted the PMA (Positive Mental Attitude) concept that was developed and introduced in 1937 by Napoleon Hill in the book *Think and Grow Rich*. I have learned by using this concept to focus my

attention on positive things throughout the day. Record in a journal daily your joyous circumstances.

7. **Don't Stop; Go Get It.** Life will always present obstacles and circumstances that seem insurmountable to manage. If you fail to manifest your passion and purpose, you will become unproductive and frustrated. Combat the enemy with your strength to endure through hardship, pain, rejection, sorrow, and failure. He has an assignment to distract you from fulfilling your purpose on earth. Don't let him. Go for the finish. Nelson Mandela said, "A winner is a dreamer who never gives up." You are a winner. You are unstoppable. Never Give up.

****BONUS*****

I also adopted *seven key decisions* when I moved from my past to my purpose that I know will help you in your journey as well. These decisions will help you remain focused.

Decision #1

I do not downsize my dreams. Valorie Burton once quoted Mark Twain in her Book "Successful Women Think differently" where he said "It isn't the things we did that we most regret, it's the thing we didn't do". (Successful Women Think Differently, Copyright 2012 Valorie Burton, Harvest House Publishers)

Decision #2

Always focus on solutions, not problems. The bigger your dream, the more opportunity for obstacles, challenges, and problems you will have. Choose a mindset that sees these problems as opportunities for growth and eventually you will walk into your vision

Decision #3

I choose to be authentic. BE YOURSELF- It takes courage, but a lot less effort.

Decision #4

I choose courage over fear. Fear is inevitable, but not a stop sign. Fear tempts you to shrink from your authentic desires.

Decision #5

I choose my relationships wisely and nurture them intentionally.

You need people, and people need you. Don't go it alone. Happiness and energy come in relationship with others.

Decision #6

I will actively seek feedback and use it to grow.

Surround yourself with people who know more than you and learn all you can from them.

Decision #7

I know my purpose and take daily action in the direction of my vision.

CONSISTENCY is key, and remember, you cannot consistently be who you are not.

Self-love was the most important instrument used to bring me from my past to my purpose. In self-love I am aware of myself and others. I understand the chameleon in me. I am self-aware and strive for self-respect, not just self-esteem. I understand that I am Unstoppable.

I love myself, I accept myself, and I cherish and protect myself. I understand that I am constantly evolving and embrace change. I found my identity again in self-love. My self-love journey is one of the best things that happened to me in life, and because I understand how important this journey is for everyone striving to move from past to purpose, I want to share my journey with you. I want you to understand how important your unconditional love for yourself is to your purpose. I want you to believe in yourself and be confident in who you are and your gifts.

What gifts do you possess that God has entrusted you with, that because you don't believe in who you are or your abilities you have not moved into yet?

Is self-concept, your perception of yourself; self-image, how you see yourself; or self-esteem, how you feel about yourself stopping you from fulfilling your purpose?

Here is one thing I know: to fulfill your purpose, you will have to know who you are, and be so confident in who you are that you don't have to explain it to others. These terms start with "self," right? Because *self* is what you must check first. You cannot serve others from an empty cup.

You must work on being the best version of yourself every day and love every version of you. Understand that each last version of you is the prerequisite for your next version.

Here are five self-destructive beliefs to get rid of as you enter an unconditional relationship with yourself.

- The belief that you have to be perfect.
- The belief that you have to be strong.
- The belief that you have to please others and that your worthiness depends on what others think of you.
- The belief that you have to hurry up and doing things quickly.
- The belief that you have to take on more responsibilities than any one person can be expected to handle.

You may be asking yourself right now how this is helping you move from your past to purpose. Here is a BIG reason; fulfilling your purpose requires the best version of you, mentally physically and emotionally. Self-love allows you to look at yourself in the mirror and check you first. It brings all the sides of you together and guides you to that better you.

<u>Meet Marie Abega</u>

 I am Marie Abega, your favorite self-Love Expert! I am a dynamic 31-year-old born in Cameroon, West Africa. I was raised in Silver Spring MD. I have lived in DC, and Virginia also. I currently reside in Houston Texas. I am the mother of two beautiful girls, Zeniah and Brielle. They are my why!

I am an Entrepreneur, Owner of Self-Love Academy Houston, Founder and President of Teenlite Inc., Black Belt Speaker, Author, and Transformational Coach and Student. After many failed relationships, disappointments, and failures, I decided to turn to myself to acquire the happiness I always felt I deserved. Join Me as I reveal my journey, and the secrets to freedom, happiness, and joy I found in my self-Love Journey.

I have a special connection with children and teen girls. My goal is to partner with as many organizations as possible that are in direct contact with young girls almost daily and spread the self-awareness and Self-love message. I believe that message have and will continue to save lives and businesses. Today, suicide is the second leading cause of death among young girls. I believe the mentoring will save lives. Mentoring saved my life. Our girls need a positive village to grow in to reach their highest potential and I believe as adults, we owe them that! Someone help you at some point, right?

My Message is simple. Know your Worth and Place your Price tag on!

My favorite affirmations are

"I AM BEAUTIFUL, INSIDE & OUT"

I AM UNSTOPPABLE

I AM ENOUGH

Connect Marie

Marie.teenliteinc@gmail.com

www.facebook.com/authorabega

www.facebook.com/teenliteinc

<u>Introducing Maureen Bobo</u>

There is no "set time" for getting over the loss of a loved one. The grief never seems to go away, and you can only hope it subsides. We try and try to put the loss in the PAST, but life has a way of reminding us that it still exists. Some people hide from it by diving into their work. Others deny the grief and put up a brave front by saying "I'm Ok" so that friends and family won't worry. Many others hide from the world altogether and suffer in silence while stuck in a past they cannot escape.

Maureen Bobo is a Grief Specialist and co-founder of the nonprofit agency, Hope for Widows Inc. She lost her husband of 10yrs suddenly, but she will be the 1st to tell you that she had lost herself long before she lost her husband. But now as a solo parent Maureen had to face her PAST in order to MOVE into the purpose she lives today. Her chapters talk about her loss of love from a young age and how that led to mistakes and mishaps as she grew into womanhood. Maureen also talks about finding herself and her GOD who helped her understand herself and reintroduce Maureen Victory is Mine Bobo to the world.

Maureen believes that GOD can use the depths of your despair to catapult you to the heights of your destiny. Keep reading this truly Unstoppable story of MOVING from PAST to PURPOSE!
~Terrance Leftridge

Chapter 11

THE NEGATIVE MERRY GO ROUND OF MY LIFE

Life is like a Big Merry-Go-Round.
You're up and then down,
Going in circles, trying to get where you are.
(Conqueror, by Estelle)

Soooo...I have this book on purpose by the great Accountability Coach Terrance Leftridge, whom we lovingly call Coach T. I'm writing my two chapters from my foundation of negativity. Have you ever felt like you were living your life from the center of a Merry-Go-Round? You could see the world spinning around you taking you thru "ups and downs", but you always felt like you stayed in virtually the same place after the ride ended. That has been my life's experience.

Everything I saw started and ended with negativity. On a merry-go-round, you will see the same things over and over again but how you see these things will determine how they affect you. Its all about perspective. So my merry-go-round started off as negative or going backward. Not because of the extreme circumstances that I experienced. I don't have that type of story. My negative thinking on my situation has shaped me.

Miscued thinking processes are VERY detrimental to the focus and trajectory of one's existence. This isn't just for those reading this piece for encouragement or direction, it's for those in charge of young minds and how they are being shaped. Your words and actions have power. PLEASE PLEASE PLEASE know that. How you see you determines how far you will go. If you SEE yourself up or if you SEE yourself down, guess what? You're correct in both "instances" Its all about you Suga Boo...

Self-Worth is so vital to your happiness. If you don't feel good about you, its hard to feel good about anything else. - Mandy Hale

For as he thinketh in his heart, so is he: - Proverbs 23:7(KJV)

UNLOVED

I can remember at the age of 3 or 4 feeling as if my father didn't want me. I believe it's the foundation of my "thinking miscues" in life. A father is a girl's first look into the mirror of the world. What he says to her and about her can shape her concept of herself for a lifetime. Just imagine if those words are negative **or nonexistence**. That young girl is left to figure out herself on her own. What if the world is giving her **a** negative view of herself and there is not a counter to that world's view. There she is, "young Maureen", left to take that seed of the world's disdain and form her opinion of her worth. That's me in a nutshell...

FLASHBACK circa early 1970ish: I ran out to hug my father one day, that same 3 or 4-year-old. He had just come home for work and I hadn't yet figured out that he didn't like me, or what my place in the world was or I don't know. What does a 4-year-old know anyway? He pushed me, away seemingly upset or disappointed or something that I understood to mean get away. That was just the beginning of what he said or didn't say or do.

It all added up to me building strongholds against myself. The patterns that developed my relationship with my father turned out to be the foundation in which I built my life's truth. See, I took those feelings of rejection, (be they true or not, because I was just a young child, nothing came to counter the feelings) and ran with it. I grew up believing that I was worthless, no one liked me, I'm ugly, I'm fat, and all things negative, just plain useless.

So then with this mindset, how do I recover? It's been a decades long battle. I mean, for me, I just retreated within myself. Why come out? Should have just gone back into the womb! I was a mama's baby anyway. I still am and she's been gone over 20 years My father never knew how his

behavior towards me was affecting me and my
wellbeing. He was a WWII veteran who grew up
in the depression era. They did things differently
back then when raising children. Plus, according to
my mother, my paternal grandmother had
attributes of stoicism also. I used that to placate
myself when I would get jealous of friends who
talk about how wonderful their father was to them.
"OH, how my father loves me" they would say. He
LOVED them so...He bought me this, He took me
here, He kissed my cheek. He smiled at me. He
acknowledged I existed... YAWN!!!... (can you see
my wishful thinking on the relationship I WISH
we could have had)

Yes, I've have the green-eyed monster on
this over the years, when others spoke on that
paternal loving relationship. I've come to the
realization that we ALL have something from our
past that can be seen as a barrier to us meeting our
destiny. It's all in the lens that you view life. If it's
cloudy then, yes, you won't see clearly. But if you
see with the lens of truth, then you can overcome
many obstacles.

My father was very dutiful and that's what
he did well.
He went to work,
He paid the bills,
I never remember utilities being shut off or
even at risk of shut off,

We had a stable home all my childhood,
We never moved.
We had STABILITY.
We were always fed, clothed,
We never worried about basic needs.

Many children would be praying for that life. I'm grateful for that from him. But my cloudy lens only allowed me to "long for" what the other kids had.

FLASHBACK mid1970ish ...Mohammad Ali was fighting SOMEBODY...does it matter???...Those of a certain era KNOW what I'm talking about. When Ali fought the world STOPPED for us...lol... My father would go in the basement and watch ABC worldwide sports (this before cable and paying for fights). He was so enthralled. I just watched. It WAS exciting. Ali won of course, and I believe that's when I turned to sports. As a little girl, I guess it wasn't supposed to be my cup of tea. I never had a tea party or really liked dolls on that level. But sports, I could get into! Maybe he would speak to me instead of grunting or telling me I did something wrong as the only communication we had. It didn't work, but I do STILL love sports. A FOREVER TOMBOY! If you want to know what happens to the tomboy that grew up, then look at me. That next day after the fight, I was excited, Ali had made me a believer in "Anything was Possible" just by the things he said and did. He had so much confidence that he would win and most of the time he was right, I loved Howard Cosell and the entire atmosphere of the fight. I went to the back yard the next day and threw a tennis ball against the house. I was going to be the next great athletic somebody with my "MAD, TALENTED tennis balls against the house skills" …

Also, I BLEED The Cleveland Browns "Brown and Orange" and my TEARS are The Cleveland Cavaliers "Wine and Gold". I think it was by design of God.

Back to my miscued thought processes...So I took my feelings of insecurity to life based on my belief that I was worthless into adolescence. I wanted to be liked and loved...

My Merry-Go-Round creaked backwards...but the music played on in the right direction...HUH??? confusion...

NOT A PARTICIPANT

Since I retreated into myself from a life of not feeling loved, a natural progression of things was for me to be isolated and alone. Growing up, it seemed as if everyone had a life but me. I would always want to be doing something or with anyone other than myself.

People were Smiling,
Kids were having fun,

217

Girls were cute and boys liked them.

I was Fat and Ugly And more FAT.
Never feeling comfortable in my own skin, I hated
me...WEIGHT do I need to say more...lol...It
weighed me down. As I grew into a young adult,
the stronghold of my worthlessness only grew into
an uncontrollable monster. At that point, I had no
antidote to the disease. Love was the answer to the
question I couldn't figure out. Nothing but pure
confusion on my part. Back then and still today, a
woman who is considered overweight is a 5th class
citizen.
> *"No one will ever want you!*
> *Why are you here!*
> *JUST DIE!!! "*

It may see extreme, but it's true. everything
negative is magnified in the mind of those who
look to the world for validation. So, WORLD, if
you're telling me "what good am I?" I believe you.
My mind was already fertile soil for "all things
negative" about me from the negative thinking
patterns already established. No Problemo...I got
the message. I would sit at home on the weekends
and listen to music, mostly Motown 70s-80s love
songs, where they sing about these great ladies of
worth that I would never be...

FLASHBACK..circa Late 1970ish: *Seems like I
just can't get close enooogh to you because I*

218

looove you so muuuch sang Ray, Goodman and Brown from (1979)...and Al Green crooned...*Love and Happiness (1972)...nuthin wroong being in looove with someone...Love and Happiness*...I didn't believe it would happen to me but I liked dreaming about it.

See with my mind already set on N for negativity, I couldn't see what I wanted the most in life. LOVE...not just a man and a woman love. That was a part of it, but it was more than that. Something was missing in me. My misery quotient has been on an all-time high for most of my life and I've felt like I was always on the outside looking in. I couldn't GET in, I didn't have a key and the door was locked. I spent most of my life trying to figure out why.

Low grade depression may be a "semi clinical term" for my state of being. All I know is that it has not served me well AT ALL. I know I'm not the only one who has felt this way. It's STRAIGHT UP!!!Bondage. But the hardest prisons to escape are the ones we create ourselves. During this time in my life of non-rediscovery of me, I'll just say it was like looking at everything you've ever wanted or needed and not being able to reach it. You CAN'T get in for some reason. You don't have the means within yourself to open the door. You spend your life on your "Merry-Go-Round" watching this scene of the candy store...NUTHIN...she stops trying and creates a life on her own terms...Life be DAMNED!!!...while still listening to Al Green (1972) and all the greats...*Hooow can you mend a BROKEN heart???...Hooow can a LOSER ever wiiiin????* Love was the key; something I desperately craved but didn't know how to reach. It was like I was a child looking through the window at a candy store I couldn't enter. I needed a locksmith...

What do you do when you believe you can't have what you desperately want???... Well for me, I just pretended it didn't matter. I pushed the desire into the deep annals of my soul and went on with life. It takes practice, and since I have a lifetime of practice on not ever getting what I wanted in life, it may have been easier for me than others. I picked myself up from my boot straps and went on to prove that I could do this sentence standing on my head. I could carry this load through life. I have been SHOT to the heart and survived...see my bullet wounds, as she slowly lifts up her shirt to show the crowd. The wound has healed but the scar remains...

I created my own disjointed sunshine of a life. Through a mutual friend, I met Martin. He was nice to me, we talked about similar things, I had nobody else, so dude, YOU get the job of TRYING to love me. He couldn't do it! Nobody could do it at that point because a man can only love a woman to the depth that she loves herself. I had no depth in that area. I won't even say we tried to make a go of it. We just did what we thought was required of us as citizens of the world. Not realizing that it was so much more to marriage than painting a pretty picture for the masses to adore...

My Merry-Go-Round slowly continued backwards. How can I get offs? Pretending I didn't care...

SENSE OF HOPELESSNESS

I didn't care about myself and I know one else did either. I was married, (but my) husband didn't care either. He did say he didn't like me quite often, so there, it's true. "Then why am I even here?" I would think. These are the natural progression of thoughts experiences that one has when living in a self-imposed life sentence of negativity. It started in childhood and just snowballed into an avalanche that didn't appear to ever going to be lifted. When I left college after 4 lonely years of struggle, I thought YES, I can now prove to the world (my father maybe???) that I am valuable.

"I got this degree and now I'm going to get a job...

Nana nana booboo (tongue stuck out at the world)
You can't tell me NUTHIN!!!..."

WRONG...I got that job and life continued to spiral downward...
This really hit home when I got to college. I thought I was all that and a bag of Cheetos educationally. I was always at the top or near top of my class from k-12 grade. I was proud of that, too proud I put it out there and wore it on my sleeve. I looked down on others who I felt were "Sub Par" because their grades weren't as good as mine. I only hung with the "Smart Kids". People tend to magnify or over exaggerate areas in their life where see themselves as strong, or they feel good, especially if the rest of their life they see as weak. OR it could be that people overcompensate just to mask their frailties.

I am not sure where I fall in this, but back then some 25 years ago, I had nothing else to make me feel secure about my place on this planet but my academic achievement. A neighbor once asked me why we weren't in the same classes at school. I remember it as clear as yesterday, I said Smugly Ugly, and Fugly as mean and ignorant as I wanna be, *"Because YOU not Smart Enough!"* I might as well had said *"YOU too dumb!"* Huh, where did I get off saying that? *"Hurt people, Hurt People"* as they say. I feel bad just writing it, but it's true.

Years later, he told me how degraded he felt when I said that. I mean Wow...I said that? How crude, and rude is an understatement. I was able to apologize, thankfully. I still regret those words. That was a negative seed I planted that I did harvest. The harvest is ALWAYS more than the seed planted. Just think of a farmer using 1 seed to plant a stalk of corn, then at the harvest about 20 corn cobs come from that seed. Seed Time and Harvest, You Bettah Recognize... and I did.

I struggled through college, at times almost failing out. I had prided myself on being smart. It was something I clung on to as my identity. Just one of those characteristics I tried to get love of my father. It didn't work...but still I loved school and learning. I patted myself on the back after every "A" in High School. Then I went to the University of Cincinnati; feeling dumb is an understatement. For one, it was culture shock. I grew up in predominantly African American, progressive, liberal, Cleveland, Ohio. Then, to go to Cincinnati which was Republican, right-conservative. Something I had not really heard of except "Reagonomics" and "Government Cheese". Plus, I was so immature, still a baby, all I needed was diapers and a bottle although I was 18. What did I know about racism, I learned to watching the mini-series," Roots" as a child. But still, "The experience is real". And for me who already was primed on being unlove, it didn't help and just added to my issues of figuring this life out that just got harder and harder by the day.

"Jesus...WHY did you ever let me go down there?" The Master shapes the clay where He wills for His purposes. "I know that's right!"

Meanwhile, I've never experienced such loneliness as when in Cincinnati. I didn't have the ability to make friends, I guess. I had a few friends in high school, but I had my parents as support. I should have never left Cleveland...smh. I spent more lonely weekends in utter pain; Emotional pain is what it was. I remember my chest literally hurting because of it.

FLASHBACK – Probably 1987-1988.

Friend: "What's Up?? Girl what you doing this weekend? I'm going to be hanging with James, we have the entire weekend planned."
Me: um not sure, we'll see.
Friend: Oh...OK! (as my classmate happily walks away into her great weekend with James.)

Me: the campus was mostly deserted, as it usually was on Friday afternoons after 4 pm. I didn't have ANYTHING planned, but 48 hours of watching TV. NOT studying for something I know I needed to study for. It was my usual MO (Modus of Operandi) at University of Cincinnati. I had a boyfriend briefly while there, but it didn't last. I wasn't ready for a relationship, had confidence issues and really couldn't connect with a person until I connected with myself.

I couldn't resolve feeling like the "Dumbest person alive" because of my GPA that was below Sea, See or C-level...whichever you want to choose. More crushing in that area, school was my stomping ground. I RULED in the classroom! It defined me. I was GREAT there! Key word being WAS...but I soon realized that I wasn't prepared for college. Cleveland Public Schools I guess. (I had to have a reason for my failure in college). Or as I think of it now, I think, I harvested my attitude towards others I thought were less than academically. I had too much pride and treated others unjustly in this area. It was unbecoming of me and I deserved my punishment for my behavior. Of course, I didn't realize it then, but after years of introspection, I've come to this conclusion. People tend to highlight were they believe their greatness lays, it's a lie because then we tend to hide instead of nurture our areas of challenge...(maureenism)

The Merry-Go-Round Sped Up going backwards... (I hope you the reader are thinking of merry-go-round sounds when reading this. Be INTERACTIVE in your literary experience!!! Don't let me do ALL the work...lol)

LACK IN EVERYTHING

I've always felt like I was not enough. "Not enough what?" you may ask. Well, when I think about it, it's not one specific thing. I just never measured up. I wasn't pretty; Not thin or rich; Always ugly; Never wanted.
"By who???"

I guess, FIRST of all, not by myself. The world CAN'T want you if you don't want yourself. I remember as a young person wanting to be anything other than me. I had to be something, somewhere better than my life. I never knew what love actually was. But yet, I always craved it. It's an interesting analyzation of my life. If I would have followed through on the suicidal ideations I had in my early to mid-20s, my epitaph could have read "UNREQUITED SELF LOVE". But thankfully, I didn't follow through, although I did cut my arms and wrist (no real blood came). I didn't make a pattern of it; it just shows how much agony I felt internally. Now I realize (see my chapter 2 for that realization), but at the time, I didn't know.

We all have within us what is necessary to grow the fruit designed for us (our divine purpose). It has to be cultivated, fertilized, fermented, and any other gardening synonym you can think of.

My goal here is to make sure you, the reader, make that realization and have some life-applicable tools to implement in your life so you don't fall into the pitfalls of life that I've fallen into. It took me 40 years to figure (this) stuff out, but a person doesn't need FORTY LONG YEARS to get on track! Please, I beg of you, don't waste that much time! There is so much work that needs to be done... One acts on what they think they can't achieve. I did, others do too. I stated earlier that I created my own disjointed reality trying to immolate happiness. In actuality, all I created was more UNHAPPINESS in my life. Why? I believe because I'm NOT the Creator. Thank God for that...lol! "I did it MY WAY" as that song says by Frank Sinatra. My way created **LACK**. Lack is the state of being without or not having enough of something. By now, I think you guys know that I lacked love and what flows from that. I believed that I didn't deserve happiness. It's surreal. **JOY** is what I wanted. Over the years, I experienced losses in (my) life; my grandmother, dear sister in law, father, mother, son, husband. Grief digs up more lack and expounds on thinking about, faith, love joy, peace and the like. A person views their own mortality and wonders about their final resting place. I was always young, it seemed. But keep living and all of a sudden, you're not.

My merry-go-round of life had been going backwards for 40 years...smh.. My husband's passing was a result of chronic heart disease; he was only 45 years old. It knocked my world off its axis. Half the time, I blamed myself because I was such a lousy wife. See, when you're on that negative, backwards merry-go-round, this is what you get. That snowball just snowballs. It doesn't break up and dissipate unless something causes it to. What could possibly do that? Martin's and my life had its ups and downs, towards the end mostly down. We had lost our son prematurely; he came too soon. It devastated us! I was just 39! We had our daughter, Jordan, who was adopted, and we loved her more than life itself. I didn't think we could conceive. We did after not really trying. But do you really have to try. No. But Jesus, It had been 12 years of marriage, no birth control. What am I supposed to think? No doctor had told me I could conceive, just that I had a bicournate uterus, misshapen I guess. Like all of my life. I took the lie that I believed after hearing that diagnosis and ran with it. My baby died...

FLASHBACK....circa 2008 We're arguing about whatever couples argue about.
Martin: "You killed OUR SON!!!.."
Me: "Why you saying that?" (Already believing it, I thought so too.)
Martin: "You should have went to the doctor earlier and recognized the symptoms."
Me: Silent, mad no comeback, tears flowing...

Ok folks, my negative backward merry-go-round needs to fix itself, plus I'm not sure you (have) ever done this but relieving some of your most negative life events to try and help people, is quite distressing, depressing and discomforting. This Puppy Needs to start Moving Forward in a positive direction...Dear reader, the point in this chapter is to give you a peak in to my view of me. My cognitive patterns were so off that I couldn't see myself ever being happy. What was happiness anyway. I did know how to spell and that was it. Misery is unbecoming as a life pattern. But often people donlt know how to break the miserable patten an dit becomes there comfort zone. People die in the comfort zone. I had had ENOUGH. I wanted to be FREE. I started hearing about people living the life of their dreams Normal, everyday people like YOU and ME.

Me: *Well...um...Jesus, I'm hearing and seeing that there's JOY in dem dere woods of the world. Its Its Its something QUITE unfamiliar to me. I'm SICK and TIRED of feeling this way. I BEG OF YOU help me LORD!!! (by this time my face is on the floor, tears streaming down) There are ACTUALLY HAPPY PEOPLE over the age of 21. Whats a gurl gotta do to GRAB HOLD of some of dat???*

Jesus: *Come to me... with His arms outstretched...I went home...*

I forgive myself for having believed for so long that I was never good enough to have, get and be what I wanted. **- Ceanne DeRohann**

PERSPECTIVE... I *always say, that if you build your thoughts on a fault line, then with the earthquake hits, and IT WILL, you hit. The lie always crumbles...I did try to make my father like me by delving into the sports that he seemed to enjoy so much. - Maureen Bobo*

Chapter 12
THE REINTRODUCTION OF MAUREEN

Hello, my name is Maureen Bobo. You first met me in my first chapter. I must admit, it wasn't all good there. I want my journey to take a permanent detour. Let's shift if to a different path. You can do that in your own life, ya know. Each day is an opportunity to make a different choice that can get you to a different destination. It's true. I had to do it and so can you.

The creaking of the merry-go-round started to change direction. Well at some point, a person has to decide. Am I going to remain here in futility? Or am I going to step forward into something, anything other than this? I don't know but there has to be more. I wanted to FEEL more than despair. I was in a turbulent place.

"They say JOY comes in the morning, but I really believe JOY comes when you choose it".
Maureen Bobo

FROM RELIGION TO RELATIONSHIP

My husband of 13 years, Martin, passed away on April 7, 2010 from chronic heart disease. He was 45 years old. Our children at the time were ages 8 years and 2 months old. We were left to make sense of the rest of our lives. The truth of the matter was that **I needed** to figure it out. Figure out how I was going to make it. Grief magnifies one's issues. I was STILL suffering from very low self-esteem, negative thought patterns and just plain ole' self-hatred. I was in a rut. A rut is nothing but a grave with both ends open. You can't get out because you're DEAD in a sense NO LIFE. The reality of it is that you can revive yourself. Resurrection, so to speak. BUT, how does one Resurrect themselves??? Glad you asked...

I've been in church since I was a young child. I'll just say "in Church" for most of my life meant going to church, sitting on the pew, saying Amen and leaving. I lived my life on my terms the rest of the week. It was a pattern I had that developed in childhood. I knew all the stories. Jesus rose, Daniel didn't get ate by the lions, the children of Israel had really bad navigational skills, David had great aim, and Mary had a baby, somehow. I'm saved. Just stories. The missing ingredient was LOVE. If it was taught, I missed that lesson...smh. I didn't have it. If you miss Love in church, in my opinion, you miss it all. It is the foundation. It was like watching a movie. I paid my fee, I accepted Christ as my savior at age 10 because they told me to. I usually did what I was told so I would not cause any problems. Obedience was not my issue. People looked over, past, around, through me most of the time. That was by design by me. On the backwards merry-go-round of life, you develop skills to manage while there. One of mine is the power of invisibility...lol...It's true. People stopped seeing me. My name was often forgotten. Becoming a widow just helped me hide more. Plus, the black I already wore all the time became even more acceptable...Cool! If a widow doesn't make a sound, does she even exist? Hmmm...Just thoughts. I say no, which is fine with someone trying to be a hidden figure anyway. But as I started to make the conscious choice to improve or as I call it "Upgrade my life", things changed. They had to...

FLASH FORWARD 2 years

TV Host: *...And here she is! That great, sought after, impressive, beautiful, motivational speaker Maureen Bobo!!! Everyone gives her a hand.*

Audience: *YEAH!!!*

I walk out to the couch for the interview.

ME: *Thank you for having me Gwen.*

TV Host: *No problem Maureen. I loved your story ever since I read it in the Unstoppable Stories book. You've inspired me and millions across the world.*

ME: *I'm so glad that my story has helped others.*
ME: *I want to say that my life changed when I made an INTENTIONAL decision to improve. I did not know how so I had to go back to the designer, the manufacturer, because the model was broken. The Creator God Himself. You see Gwen, so many times we want to do it all ourselves.*

TV Host: *Do tell.*

ME: *Well we want to control it all. We want it our way, or the high way. When it should be Yahweh or no way.*

(Audience laughs).

TV Host: *That is so true Maureen, why do you think so many people lose their way in life?*

ME: *I believe, at least for me, it all boiled down to a Love Lack Condition. If you don't have it, you don't have it, love that is. It's apparent and it shows. Everybody knows it. You may not know your problem, but the One who made you can fix it. I had to get service from the master technician. He puts you through the processing plant for* *growth. That entails spending time with Him for rediscovery and direction. What I call marinating in His Word. Get some understanding in prayer fellowship with mature, loving Christians, and self-esteem. Find out that you are fearfully and wonderfully made, a chosen person, part of a grand inheritance, formed before the foundations of the earth saved by grace, loved with an everlasting love...Hallelujah Gwen, I'm getting excited just talking about it.*

TV Host: *Me too, but first we need to go to commercial break to pay some bills.*

(Audience laughs)

TV Host: *I see Maureen, we are going to have to have you back for more inspiration...*

ME: *Anytime Gwen, anytime...*

Fade back to present...

My merry-go-round slowly speeds up in the right direction. I realize that it's my thoughts that control it. What you and I say, do, see, believe and feel about ourselves is true. We create our reality. Therefore, if we are creating our reality, we might as well make it great.

A. Problem Solving - Tip Take Note

1. **Seek God:** But seek ye first the kingdom of God, and his righteousness; and all these things shall be added unto you. **(Matthew 6:33)** *KJV*
2. **Memorize Scripture**: This book of the law shall not depart out of thy mouth; but thou shalt meditate therein day and night, that thou mayest observe to do according to all that is written therein: for then thou shalt make thy way prosperous, and then thou shalt have good success. **(Joshua 1:8)** *KJV*
3. **Speak Life over your life:** Death and life are in the power of the tongue: and they that love it shall eat the fruit thereof. **(Proverbs 18:21)** *KJV*

B. Self-Development Takes – (because people learn how they learn)

1. **Napoleon Hill** – Cherish your visions and your dreams as they are the children of your soul, the blueprints of your ultimate achievements.
2. **Ralph Waldo Emerson** – What lies behind us and what lies before us are tiny matters compared to what lies within us.
3. **Rainer Maria Rilke** - The only journey is the one within

THE DESIRE FOR CHANGE

A few months after Martin passed away, I started asking myself "Who Am I?" I mean I'd been with him for 17 years; married for 13. I only knew me as a wife, mother and employee. That's it. What was my place in the world? Whom could I turn to? I disconnected and isolated myself (not recommended). When you get alone with your thoughts, then your thoughts tend to lean negative, unless you have a pattern of positive thinking. I didn't have those positive thoughts yet. I started to think that God didn't create me for a lifetime of misery. I had to change. Once you decide to change, then the next step is HOW to change? The same routines, patterns and habits WILL NOT DO. You are making a NEW you.

The merry-go-round continued in a nice forward moving pace. She started smiling.

Now we already established that we could resurrect ourselves, next is the change.

FLASH FORWARD 5 years

CROWD GOING CRAZY: *YEAA!!!, YEAH!!!, YESS!!!*

ANNOUNCER: *Here she comes, everybody's favorite Half Marathoner. The ONE and ONLY the GREAT FLO BOBO!!! YEAHHH!!!...*

Bells ringing,
CROWD CHANTS:
FLO!!!...FLO!!!...FLO!!!...FLO!!!...FLO!!!.

*(I come around the bend of the stadium. I'm Finishing ACTUALLY running my 25th Half Marathon and 15th state. With a goal to run a half marathon in every state, 35 more to go YES! for those who are counting WHOPEEE! I finally got it. GOT WHAT? IT!! me I FOUND my JOY! Deeeeep Euphoria. Training, Running, Walking Cardio, Strength work, managing food intake, all of it. Sponsors all around, product reviews, Nike's calling, YES NIKE! Is calling Flo because she's a REAL person who happens to be an athlete. There are millions of people just like her all over the world. Milli*ons of people who are inspired by her from TRAGEDY to TRIUMPH story. Write it down. You were a witness to her greatness...)*

(Oh yeah, for those who don't know, Flow Bobo is my athletic alter ego, UNLEASHED!!! by God around 2014. She had been lying dormant since I was about 6 or 7. Remember back in my first chapter when I was the "greatest tennis ball against the house" player after the Ali fight? That was the birth of Flo Bobo then. She loves all things

sports and competition. She's my Health and wellness ministry and self-care advocate.)

Back to the finish line:

YOUNG WIDOW: *Flo, can I get a picture with you?*

ME: *Why sure.*

YOUNG WIDOW: *You inspire me so. My husband passed away 2 years ago, and I have been lost. But following your story of how you picked yourself up after your husband died has helped me see that I CAN go on. (((HUGS))).*

ME: *I'm so glad but please remember, It's not me, It's He. I'm just a vessel....*

Back to now...

I started working out in 2011. It was just to lose some weight. However, it became more than that. The workouts are like my worship. I'm taking care of the temple, eating mostly vegetarian and just really conscious of my emotional, mental, and physical self. That's change. Taking small steps. You don't have to run a half marathon, but you do have to start...Hmmm that sounds like the workings of another book...lol...

My merry-go-round rounded forward in a nice steady jog.

Take Note

But they that wait upon the Lord shall renew their strength; they shall mount up with wings as eagles; they shall run, and not be weary; and they shall walk, and not faint. **(Isaiah 40:31)** *KJV*

9 What? know ye not that your body is the temple of the Holy Ghost which is in you, which ye have of God, and ye are not your own? For ye are bought with a price: therefore glorify God in your body, and in your spirit, which are God's. **(1 Corinthians 6:19-20)** *KJV*

I beseech you therefore, brethren, by the mercies of God, that ye present your bodies a living sacrifice, holy, acceptable unto God, which is your reasonable service. And be not conformed to this world: but be ye transformed by the renewing of your mind, that ye may prove what is that good, and acceptable, and perfect, will of God. **(Romans 12:1-2)** *KJV*

Self-Development Takes

Virgil - The Greatest Wealth is health
Healthy is not a goal it's a way of living
(Unknown)
Leigh Hunt – The Groundwork of all happiness is
health.
Jim Rohn – Take care of your body, it's the only
place you have to live.

<u>DISCOVERING MY IDENTITY</u>

I found myself when I learned how to love
myself. It seems odd, but it's true. How does one
know who they truly are unless they do some real
self-introspection? People don't do that unless they
care to know who they actually are. The research
on self comes with love of one's self. I found me
when I started to see myself through the lens of
God. God was my optometrist because my glasses
had an incorrect prescription that needed to be
fixed. My glasses were cloudy with the chance of
more cloudiness. I'm sure I'm not the only one. I'll
just say the road to clarity is paved with the tears
of your experiences...

FLASHFORWARD 4 years

TYNDALE HOUSE: *Well Ms. Bobo, what do you
think?*

ME: *I don't know what to say. I'm speechless. Your offer is so so so very generous. A contract and stipend for the release of my next 5 books? WOW! I wasn't expecting...*

(Oh, STOP IT! You're doing a FLASHFORWARD on this, so that denotes that you DID expect this...lol... I signed the contract with Tindale House.)

Point being, visualization is very important in success planning. I guess that's what we're doing. No, I KNOW that's what we're doing. You bought this book to get a resource to help you make improvements in your life so that you can be more successful. SUCCESS PLANNING!!!...You're Welcome.

(You have to see it to bring it to you. Whatever your IT is. Be specific and detailed. This will also help you set clear, concise goals. You have to believe you can do it. Focus like a laser beam on it, and then implement a plan with action steps. Gaze with positive emotions at what you desire in life several times a day. Write positive affirmations to repeat over and over in your head and aloud. Pray to be aligned with God's will in your life. You want your dreams to be fueled by God's power.)

I will make $50000 OR MORE a month with my business.
PROSPERITY and FAVOR are my daily companions.
I have opportunities for MULTIPLE STREAMS, LAKES and OCEANS of income constantly coming to me.
I am in CONTINUAL UPGRADE MODE, growing and improving in all areas of my life.
I have LOVING friends and family who are a positive SUPPORT SYSTEM in my life.
I ENHANCE and bring VALUE to everyone I connect with.

You can make about 20 or more affirmations to speak over your life. Have fun with it. Enjoy...

Start Here
Trust in the Lord with all thine heart; and lean not unto thine own understanding. In all thy ways acknowledge him, and he shall direct thy paths.**Proverbs 3:5-6** *KJV*
Delight thyself also in the Lord: and he shall give thee the desires of thine heart.. **Psalm 37:4** *KJV*
And we know that all things work together for good to them that love God, to them who are the called according to his purpose. **Romans 8:28** *KJV*

Self-Development Takes

Visualization is Daydreaming with a Purpose –
Robert Foster Bennett

Create the highest grandest vision possible for
your life, because your become what you believe –
Oprah Winfrey

It takes someone with the vision of the possibilities
to attain new levels of experience. Someone with
the courage to live his dreams. –
Les Brown
What is guided imagery?

Guided imagery is a program of directed
thoughts and suggestions that guide your
imagination toward a relaxed, focused state. You
can use an instructor, tapes, or scripts to help you
through this process.

Guided imagery is based on the concept that
your body and mind are connected. Using all of
your senses, your body seems to respond as though
what you are imagining is real. An example often
used is to imagine an orange or a lemon in great
detail-the smell, the color, the texture of the peel.
Continue to imagine the smell of the lemon, and
then see yourself taking a bite of the lemon and
feel the juice squirting into your **mouth**. Many
people salivate when they do this.

This **exercise** demonstrates how your body

can respond to what you are imagining.

You can achieve a relaxed state when you imagine all the details of a safe, comfortable place, such as a beach or a garden. This relaxed state may aid healing, learning, creativity, and performance. It may help you feel more in control of your emotions and thought processes, which may improve your attitude, health, and sense of well-being.

https://www.webmd.com/balance/stress-management/tc/guided-imagery-topic-overview

My forward moving merry-go-round continued at a steady pace, visualizing herself as a double decker, with a real live calliope (steam organ) player on board...VISION!!!

WALKING IN PURPOSE

Well everybody, we're here. Ahhh Purpose. We walked through a synopsis of my pain, discussed some points to take or lessons learned, life application. I hope you took note and were somewhat entertained. You see it all boils down to love. Your value statement on you. You have to hold yourself in the highest of esteem to get what you want out of life. I believe we all are here for a reason. In the Christian Faith, once you become a believer, your purpose for Kingdom advancement starts to form. You may not know right away, but over time it should become more evident. For me it has become clear. Some of my assignments or roles are my MINISTRY! I know. I'm a woman, parent, social worker, health and wellness advocate, grief recovery.

I've Coauthored/Collaborated on 4 books, *The Unwelcome Committee, Grief Diaries: Poetry, Prose and More, Widowed but not Wounded: The Hustle and Flow of 13 Black Widowed Women.* I speak on my grief journey. I'm also the Co-director of Hope for Widows Foundation, a 501c3 organization that assists widows through grief with peer to peer support, initiatives, activities and programs that enhances their healing. We already talked about Flo Bobo. I think all that speaks of PURPOSE.

But I'm also single, or I say sometimes jokingly say SANGLE as a DOLLA BILL! lol. Truthfully, I refer to this season in my life as solo. To me solo denotes completeness. For example, something that is single, can always be improved with addition. If you had the choice to choose 1 dollar or double it to 2 dollars, I think most would choose the 2 dollars because it is worth more than the 1 dollar.

If I listen to a soloist, especially if she is a great singer, she is complete. She wouldn't be improved if you add another singer to make it a duet. In fact, you may downgrade the song. Not that an arrangement couldn't be made to make her song into a duet, but it would change it and not necessarily make it better. The point being is that the soloist is complete. The dollar is not to me. I look at myself as complete. So, anything added to me will only enhance me, not make me better. I hope that makes sense.

Meanwhile, God had to work with me in the processes of singleness. It's been almost 8 years and my perspective has definitely changed. I went from "Why me Lord to Here I am Lord, Use me!!!" in my singleness. I've found solitude, which to me is being alone with peace. It's a tranquil, serenity wrapped in peace. Close your eyes and just imagine a beautiful place of calm. That's my solitude in my singleness right now. It's the result of spending time with God where I listen to Him. It's when He called me to singleness. Yes, I was called.

Yes, I became single when my husband passed away, but there was a specific time when I realized that there was more to it. IT wasn't all about me. God had a plan for me. PURPOSE! I had to get close to Him. No, I didn't want to be here experiencing the circumstance that got me here, but I'm here writing this chapter, speaking to you the reader about my experience, helping someone be encouraged in their own singles walk.

FLASHFORWARD 6 months -3 YEARS and beyond...

PASTOR: *Thank you choir...Now everyone, God has blessed us with a special guest speaker. Maureen Bobo is here this morning to speak to the congregation on the importance of Singles Ministry and singles being nurtured in their season of singleness in life. She has worldwide recognition and is often sought after for speaking on this topic. She has written a book with contracts in the works for more projects. There is even talk of a play coming out. Amen!! She lives her life for Christ and all who hear her are truly blessed. She has taken the time out of her busy schedule to be utilized as a vessel for God to impart wisdom that He has spoken to her. And I heard that Oprah was calling her y'all. HALLELUJAH!!! Plus, there are rumors that there is a somebody out there "IN THE AIR" in her life.*

Crowd laughs

Let's give a warm welcome for Maureen Bobo!!!...

My merry-go-round slows down, starting to stop to let the riders off. She inwardly smiled knowing that she accomplished what she was meant to. She waits expectantly for the next group to bless...

Versus for Singles

I charge you, O ye daughters of Jerusalem, by the roes, and by the hinds of the field, that ye stir not up, nor awake my love, till he please. **Song of Solomon 3:5** *KJV*
But let it be the hidden man of the heart, in that which is not corruptible, even the ornament of a meek and quiet spirit, which is in the sight of God of great price. **1 Peter 3:4**. *KJV*

Self-Development for singles

The women who doesn't require validation from anyone is the most feared individual on the planet – **Mohadesa Najumi**

Some steps need to be taken alone, its the only way to figure out where you need to be. **Mandy Hale**

Trust the wait, embrace the uncertainty, enjoy the beauty of becoming. When nothing is certain, anything is possible. - **Mandy Hale**

Farmers love fertile soil, always be ready for cultivation – **Maureen Bobo**

Thank YOU, dear reader, for your desire for improvement. Huh??? YOU may think. Yes, YOU are doing a great job. YOU have made a conscious effort to do something for yourself to make your tomorrows thank YOU for today. It speaks to your TENACITY...DRIVE...and DETERMINATION to reach your highest self. KUDOS to YOU!!!!

Also, I wanted to let you know that I enjoyed sharing my story with you and offer ways to connect with me as I venture into other projects to elevate those who follow me. Below are some ways to connect with me:

I am available for speaking engagements, training for corporate, church, school, home and individually. The topics can vary to the need of the audiences I speak to.

Facebook: MaureenVictoryisMine Bobo
Twitter: Maureen Bobo
Instagram: maureenboboministries
Email: rebeccaschild@aol.com

As I mentioned earlier, I am a Co-director of Hope for Widows Foundation (www.hopeforwidows.org). We offer peer to peer support for the healing processes of widows. If you know of a widow that could utilize resources for healing and connection with other widows, we have a

Facebook Fanpage -

https://www.facebook.com/hope4widows/

AND

A closed group for women only who are widows

You can email us at

www.hopeforwidows@gmail.com

Books I've Coauthored/Contributed to:

The Unwelcome Committee is available on Amazon with Kindle download availability:
http://amzn.to/2Fje7ta

Grief Diaries: Poetry, Prose and More:
http://amzn.to/2ByWYty

Widowed but not Wounded: The Hustle and Flow of 13 Widowed Black Women:
http://amzn.to/2DGfPIW

STAY TUNED for more on **SINGLENESS** in my next book...

I end whatever I do with the following:

*I **LOVE** you I **LOVE** you I **LOVE** you...Be Blessed...MUAH!!!*

Maureen

P.S. Thanks Coach T for the opportunity. (((HUGS)))...:)

<u>Meet Maureen Bobo</u>

 Maureen Bobo is a Christ Follower, Love Advocate, Speaker, Author, Social Worker, Mother and Entrepreneur. Maureen is a solo parent of two daughters ages fifteen and eight. She became a solo parent on April 7, 2010, when her husband of thirteen years, Martin Quinn Bobo, passed away of chronic heart disease at the age of forty-five. The children at that time were ages eight years and two months old. The grief from that tragedy led Maureen to develop The Beautiful Stones Ministries, in which the goal is to provide love and support to the grieving heart through grief support groups and social services. Maureen is a Co-Director of Hope for Widows Foundation, a 501c3 organization that implements activities, programs and initiatives for widows to enhance their healing processes after the loss of their spouse. Maureen is a co-author of 'The Unwelcome Committee'; the story of three young widows with children and their navigation through the processes of grief. Maureen is a Contributor to Grief Diaries: Poetry Prose and More, a heartfelt collection of expressive writing from poets, journalers and bloggers. Maureen is a contributor to Widowed but not Wounded: The Hustle and Flow of 13 Resilient Black Widowed Women. Maureen is also involved

in singles ministry development at her church. She believes that singles need to be nurtured and cultivated in the season that they are in so they can thrive in God's purposes for their lives. Maureen has completed five half marathons and has a goal to complete a half marathon in every state. She has a message for people: "Be your own superhero and make your own self proud through intentional self-care." and that you CAN go from "Tragedy to Triumph." Although based in Ohio, Maureen plans to encourage people worldwide to rock their inner athlete to the core and become unleashed! Through her life story, Maureen wants to encourage and inspire people to not only dream but dream big, by putting their faith in flight and loving themselves and others. Maureen is available for speaking, training, teaching engagements on various topics she has a plethora of life experience that would add value and enhance the lives of those listening. Reach out to her at: **rebeccaschild@aol.com**